TRUE LOVE LASTS

"This book can help a person find something that can't be bought - true love."

This book is dedicated to my Mom and Dad in appreciation of their unconditional love for me and for their commitment to each other during 62 years of marriage.

If you have the "I pretty much know it all about healthy relationships, I don't need to read any book" attitude, please immediately read Chapter 22 before it's too late.

"It's amazing how little preparation most people do to get ready for a healthy relationship. It's almost like they don't realize that when they date, who they date, and how they date will have a lot to do with whether or not they'll find true love and their future happiness."

"Most people make dating choices mainly based upon liking someone, feelings, and looks. It's no wonder that so many people eventually get their heart broken - and only about 6 out of every 100 (6%) marriages last 50 years."

Dear prospective reader of *True Love Lasts*,

A good number of people read the first few pages of a book to decide whether or not it's worth reading. If you decide not to read it, this might be my only opportunity to communicate some important information to you about healthy relationships. So let me highlight the main points that I explain in more detail later in the book:

1. Many teens and young adults start dating before they're ready and use the disastrous weak approach to dating in which dating choices are made mainly based upon liking someone, feelings, and looks. Unfortunately, this approach usually leads to a broken heart

2. A good amount of time and effort needs to be put into preparing yourself for a healthy relationship

3. If you prepare yourself for a healthy relationship by learning when, who, and how to date - you're more likely to make good dating choices and have a lifelong loving marriage

4. It's important that you become a strong person before you start dating and that you only date another strong person

5. If at all possible, you should try to find a way to get to know someone before dating and you should be very selective about who you decide to date

6. Dating should be a slow process in which you carefully discover what the person you're dating is really like - and whether or not he or she possibly is the person that you want to be married to for the rest of your life

7. Long make out sessions during dating and sex before marriage can be harmful to you and to your future for several important reasons - including the fact that these activities often cause an emotional attachment to develop too quickly in a relationship and they increase the likelihood that a person will ignore serious problems in the person they're dating

8. Many people don't realize that getting the feeling of being "in love" is relatively easy - especially during dating

9. Having the feeling of being "in love" makes people ignore danger signs and serious problems in their significant other - problems that could destroy a healthy relationship

10. True love is much more than just having the feeling of being "in love" - it's supposed to be a lifelong commitment

11. Having the feeling of being "in love" and having true love aren't good enough reasons alone to get married

12. Way too many people decide to get married without going through a careful marriage decision making process and they end up getting married too quickly for the wrong reasons - usually with unhappiness and divorce as the result

13. Marrying a person who isn't a hard worker almost always is a big mistake

14. Statistics show that waiting to get married until age 24 significantly decreases the likelihood of divorce

15. The amount of unhappiness in marriage and the divorce rate could be significantly reduced if couples would put in more effort to keep the feeling of being "in love" at a high level

16. The first step toward finding a person with whom you could eventually have a lifelong loving marriage is to become the type of person that you want to date - a strong person

I hope that you decide to read the book.

TRUE LOVE LASTS

A GUIDE TO HEALTHY RELATIONSHIPS FOR TEENS AND YOUNG ADULTS

JAMES WEGERT, M.ED.
SCHOOL COUNSELOR

Strong Book Publishing
Lancaster, PA

ISBN-13: 978-0-9899152-0-5

Library of Congress Control Number: 2013949393

Printed and bound in the United States of America.

TABLE OF CONTENTS

INTRODUCTION

"Why should I take the time to read this book? I'm busy!"

This book has three really important goals. The first one is to provide practical information that you can use to prepare yourself for a healthy relationship. The second is to make it more likely that one day you'll find true love. The third goal is to help reduce the number of broken hearts and the divorce rate in our society by starting a cultural revolution in regard to the approach to dating that most people use.

In order to start achieving these goals I'm going to give you information/suggestions about dating and things related to dating that I wish I'd known when I was a teen and a young adult. I developed this material using the bad choices that I've made in my life, the bad choices that I've seen so many others make in their lives, my education, and research.

I tried to pack as much useful information as possible into this book because as a school counselor I couldn't just sit back anymore and watch people mess up their lives by making bad dating choices without trying to do more to help.

Please accept my warning in advance that you may not like some of what you read. At times you may feel like yelling and tearing the book to pieces. My request is that you take the time to read it from cover to cover, even if you don't agree with some of it. Please use what makes sense to have the best possible life.

This book wasn't written to be read once and then forgotten - it was written to be referred back to over and over again - think of it as a guide or a roadmap for dating. Isn't it a good idea to have a map before you go on a road (dating) that you've never been on before, that you haven't been on long, or that you're somewhat lost on? Well here goes . . .

Look around you; the health of many relationships between men and women isn't good. Lots of people are dating before they're ready and are making dating choices mainly based upon whether or not they like someone, feelings, and looks - instead of waiting to date until they've become a strong person and only dating another strong person (explained later). Some people are in an emotionally and/or physically abusive dating relationship and they don't understand that a healthy dating relationship is based upon mutual respect. A large number of people don't think that having a lifelong loving marriage relationship is even possible. The number of couples living together without being married is at an all-time high. Many people marry with a selfish "as long as I have the feeling of being in love" commitment instead of an "as long as we both shall live" commitment. (In other words, they don't have true love for each other as explained in Chapter 16.) Millions of married couples are unhappy because they don't have the fulfilling healthy relationship that they hoped for. The divorce rate is way too high. These facts are proof that our society isn't doing enough to help and motivate people to really prepare themselves for a healthy relationship.

In addition to giving you information/suggestions, my hope is that *True Love Lasts* will help you to paint a picture in your mind of how wonderful a lifelong loving marriage could be . . . and that by picturing it; you'll be motivated to do whatever it takes to prepare yourself for a healthy relationship.

Contrary to what many people think, preparing yourself for this type of relationship is going to take a good amount of time, effort, and learning as well as personal growth. Although it won't be easy, the possible rewards if you decide to get married one day are great - rewards like having a husband or wife:

- with whom you have a close loving relationship

- who's your best friend

- who tries their best to treat you with kindness, tenderness, love, and respect in their thoughts, words, and actions on a daily basis

- who loves you unconditionally just the way you are

- who tries their best to meet your emotional, physical, social, and financial needs

- who doesn't cheat on you

- with whom you can resolve differences in a calm constructive manner

- who wants only the best for you

- with whom you have the strong feeling of being "in love" (most of the time) and with whom you have true love

- with whom you can share the joys of children

- with whom you have a 40, 50, or 60-year loving marriage

As you read this book please keep in mind that even though I may sound like a "know it all" at times, I realize that I don't have all of the answers and that I'm still learning. My hope is that the information I've written will help you to avoid bad dating choices that can mess up your life.

Before, during, or after dating I wish I'd known . . .

Question: "Why is it so hard to find a 'good' man or a 'good' woman to date?"

My opinion is that our society just isn't producing enough "good" men and "good" women. I believe that one of the reasons for this is that we're not doing a good enough job helping people learn how to become strong. We need to do a much better job of teaching people how to make good choices and to not be concerned about what weak people say, do, or think. We're not showing people that there's a better way to live their lives than following the crowd and doing what other people are doing in order to fit in and be accepted. We're also letting the false message promoted by the media and our popular culture that selfishness is the way to fulfillment and happiness drown out the message that a person is more likely to find these things if they become a strong person and get off of themselves by focusing on caring about others. My hope is that this book will help to produce more "good" men and "good" women by providing some useful information - including the fact that living your life as a strong person is more exciting and fulfilling than living your life mainly for personal gain and personal pleasure.

**"Every person is a unique treasure, more valuable than silver or gold - even if they don't have fame, lots of money, a great personality, or good looks. Don't believe anyone who says otherwise."**

1

... OUR SOCIETY HAS LOTS OF PEOPLE WITH SERIOUS PROBLEMS

"Carefully use dating to find out if they exist"

As a teen and young adult, I didn't realize that lots of people have some type of serious problem. I mistakenly thought that most people were raised in a home like mine - a home in which they were given firm, fair, kind, and consistent discipline by parents who loved them. Little did I know that were many parents who didn't really care about being a good parent, who didn't know that permissive parenting (letting their child pretty much do whatever they feel like doing) makes it more likely that their child will develop a serious problem, or who didn't have the parenting skills and/or the strength needed to bring up their children right.

When parents don't do a good job of parenting, it has a negative effect upon their children and on generations to come. Children who aren't taught how to have good character, how to display a positive attitude, how to fulfill their responsibilities, how to give their best effort, and how to demonstrate self-control usually don't know how to raise their children well - and the cycle continues to the next generation.

Violence, greed, selfishness, alcohol and other drug abuse, sex before marriage, having children without being married, unhappiness in marriage, divorce - all of these things in our society could be reduced if more parents did a good job of fulfilling their responsibilities.

You might be saying to yourself, "What does all of this have to do with a healthy relationship?" It's very important for your sake that you don't end up dating or marrying a person who has one or more serious problems. Unfortunately, many people who have serious problems (such as selfishness, dependency, anger, untreated mental health conditions, disrespect toward others, irresponsibility, lack of integrity, dishonesty, laziness, careless spending, a desire to control you, an unwillingness to grow up, and addictions to alcohol and other drugs, pornography, gambling, etc.) will try to hide their problems from you during dating. They'll make every effort to only show you their good side. When humans have the feeling of being "in love" and they're dating a person who seems to have everything that they want (looks, personality, money, etc.) - they usually ignore or minimize the importance of serious problems, problems that often destroy a marriage. Bluntly, if you end up marrying a person with a serious problem, your life could become a living hell. For example, if you marry a person who has a hidden anger problem, almost always their hidden anger will eventually come out on you. It happened to me (more about that later).

The purpose of this chapter is to warn you that many people who seem to have it all together have hidden serious problems that you need to try to discover before dating and during dating. Please don't set yourself up for disaster by sugarcoating or overlooking a serious problem in the person who you're dating (for example, by saying to yourself what I've heard over and over again from people I counsel - something like, "Yes it's true that he can't get along with lots of people including his mother, but he's *so* nice to me - and that's all that matters.")

Reflection: What are the dangers of dating someone who has a serious problem?

2

2

... WE LIVE IN A WAR ZONE WITH BRAINWASHED PEOPLE

"The forces of evil want your heart and mind"

When I was your age, I didn't realize that I was living in a war zone with brainwashed people. Yeah, I know it sounds crazy, like I'm out of my mind - but I'm completely serious. And the war zone today is even more dangerous now than it was then.

The war zone I'm talking about isn't like the one you see in the movies, on TV, or on the news with people shooting at each other - it's a war zone in your heart and mind between the forces of good and the forces of evil. (I know it still sounds a bit wacko, but hear me out.)

It's crucial for you to understand that you're being bombarded by evil influences that want to control your heart and mind. For example, the content of many magazines, books, movies, the internet, TV shows, and music isn't good - in fact, some of it is pure garbage.* It glamorizes things like looks, getting as much stuff as you can for yourself, cursing, gossip, alcohol and other drug use, violence, lust, and sex before marriage. I realize that things from the media may be exciting to read, watch or listen to for the moment, but you need to know that they damage your heart and mind. This is especially true for males who watch or see garbage, because they can visualize what they've seen for a long, long time - it's almost as if it gets permanently burned into their brain. Sadly, if I want to, I can still visualize one of the first pornographic pictures that I was shown by a "friend" when I was in fifth or sixth grade. So don't believe anyone who says, "Yeah, I look at, watch, and listen to that stuff - but it doesn't have any effect on me." They're fooling themselves.

3

(Research shows that viewing pornography negatively changes how the brain works.)

The truth is that it's not good to fill up your head with garbage. You need to know that the reason so much garbage is being produced by the media is because garbage sells. Do you understand that many people are trying to put garbage into your head in order to make money? In other words, they're taking advantage of you for their own personal gain. They know that the value systems of many teens and young adults aren't solidly formed. They're trying to impose their value system upon you; they want you to think that bad choices are OK so they'll be able to sell you more garbage in the future. They could care less about you as a person and the negative effect that watching or listening to their garbage has upon your heart and mind.

In regard to brainwashing - the definition of brainwashing is something like, "forcing someone to have certain attitudes or beliefs." Do you think that the constant daily barrage of the media has brainwashed many people into thinking that things like pornography, having sex before marriage, drinking, and gambling are OK? The media has a way of making things that are bad choices and that will damage or destroy your life, seem like harmless fun with no consequences. I urge you to take whatever steps are necessary to protect your heart and mind from the negative influence of the media (which means that you need to be strong and really limit what you hear and see - for example, refuse to listen to music, read magazines and books, visit internet sites, watch TV shows, or go to movies that glamorize things that you know are bad choices).

Unfortunately it seems that many of us have also been brainwashed by the media and our popular culture to believe that there's only one approach to dating. Specifically, the message from the media and our popular culture that we receive over and over again every day is that when a person wants to start dating all they need to do is use the approach of searching for a person with looks, personality, and possibly money who they like, who they have feelings for, who they are attracted to - so that they can "fall in love" with them. Since we see people start romantic relationships using this approach over and over again in movies and on TV, hear about romantic relationships using this approach all the time in music, read about people using this approach in books and magazines, and see our friends starting romantic relationships using this approach (and so far it seems to be working) - we really believe the fairy tale that all we have to do is search for a person who has everything we want and be ready to "fall in love and live happily ever after." I made the bad choice of using this approach to dating.

Unfortunately, this approach has several major problems. The first problem is that it's based upon selfishness - can you see it? A person using this approach is just trying to get what they want for themselves. The second problem is that the result of using this approach is usually heartbreak. In fact, over the past one hundred years, the number of broken hearts from using this approach is in the billions - and sadly even after having their heart broken, most people use the same approach again and again simply because they don't know what else to do. The third problem with this approach is that it promotes that being lazy is OK - it basically says that a person doesn't have to do much of anything to prepare themselves for dating - just be searching and be ready because you never know when you're going to "fall in love." Doesn't this approach sound a lot like gambling? In fact, part of its allure is that it's kind of mysterious and exciting. But just like gambling, the odds of winning (having a lifelong loving marriage) by using this approach are stacked against you. People are rolling the dice by making bad dating choices without really thinking and hoping that the dice don't come up "snake eyes" (a broken heart or worse).

Isn't it unbelievably sad that so many people use an approach to dating that's based upon a fairy tale, selfishness, and laziness, that's a lot like gambling, and that usually doesn't work?

Based upon this information, let's call this approach what it is - it's the weak approach to dating. I'll explain Strong Dating™, a real alternative to the weak approach, in Chapter 15.

*I've been amazed at the power that music seems to hold over people. When we play a popular song in our school auditorium almost everyone seems to be singing along because they've heard the song so many times and the tune is catchy. Unfortunately the words of many of these songs encourage people to use the weak approach to dating and to make other bad choices.

Reflection: How have the media and our popular culture influenced your planned approach to dating or the approach to dating that you're currently using?

"Right is right, even if everyone is against it, and wrong is wrong, even if everyone is for it."
- William Penn

3

. . . DIVORCE IS DEVASTATING OUR SOCIETY

"People who say that divorce is no big deal simply don't know what they're talking about"

When I was young I didn't think much about divorce. It didn't seem to happen very often and when it did, it wasn't talked about. Man, have times changed - for the worse. Everywhere you go and in the media you hear about people getting divorced. Divorce, something that used to be rare, seems to be happening all the time. Now it's almost accepted as something that's "no big deal", that's "OK", that "just happens", and that "there's not much we can do about it."

It's true that divorce has become a pandemic in our society. I didn't know what a pandemic was until I looked it up in the dictionary - it said, pandemic: something affecting a very high number of people. The statistics out there are a bit confusing - but most sources seem to agree that at the very least 30% of all marriages (almost 1 in every 3 marriages) end in divorce. That sounds very high to me.

Let's put it this way, if divorce was a disease, and 30% of all married people caught it, do you think that we'd be sitting around saying, "It's no big deal, it's OK, it just happens, and there's not much we can do about it?" No, we'd be educating people about how to avoid catching it, we'd being doing tons of research about it, we'd have public service announcements about it on TV, on the radio, and on billboards - who knows we might even hold walkathons or dance marathons to raise funds to help prevent it.

I know that statistics can be boring, but let me give you one more that surprised me:

- only about 6% of all people who get married end up having a 50-year marriage - that's only 6 out of every 100 couples

So why doesn't our society take more action and do whatever it can to minimize divorce? I'm not sure, but let me take a few guesses:

- Could it be that many of us know couples who used the weak approach to dating and they have a happy marriage?

- Could it be that some of us know people (maybe even ourselves) who are currently using this approach to dating and so far everything seems great?

- Could it be that many of us believe that the weak approach to dating is the only approach?

- Could it be that many of us think there's not much preparation work that needs to be done prior to dating in order to minimize the possibility of divorce?

- Could it be that we don't really want anybody giving us suggestions about our love life and we don't feel comfortable giving anyone else suggestions about their love life?

- Could it be that some of us have the "Divorce won't happen to me" attitude? I confess that I used to have that attitude . . . until it happened to me. (I'll share my painful story later in the book. If you have this attitude right now please immediately turn to p. 89.)

- Could it be that many of us believe that there's nothing that can be done to reduce divorce?

- Could it be that we don't realize how many people's lives are affected by divorce? The Census Bureau says that the number of divorced people has mushroomed from about 4 million in 1970 to almost 20 million in the year 2000.

Shockingly, 50% of all children will live with only one of their parents sometime during their childhood and this missing parent is usually the dad . . . 50% of all children, oh my . . . and we wonder why the world is such a mess. As a school counselor in several inner city schools, I've seen the negative effects that having only one parent can have upon some students. They're missing a role model that they desperately need and their behavior tends to spin out of control more easily.

- Could it be that we don't really understand the effects of divorce?

Of course there are the initial effects of divorce such as incredible stress, pain, shock, confusion, anger, grief, and uncertainty. But research shows that divorce also has long lasting negative effects in many cases - for example:

Depression - Children of divorced parents are about seven times more likely to suffer from depression in adult life than people of similar age and background whose parents have not divorced. The loss of a parent through divorce is more likely to cause depression than loss through death

High school dropouts - Teens whose parents are divorced are more likely to drop out of high school than those who have married parents (and the majority of people in prison are high school dropouts)

Drug use - over 70% of adolescents in drug rehabilitation hospitals are from single parent families

Suicide - over 60% of suicides are individuals from single parent families

Teenage pregnancies - over 70% of teenage pregnancies are adolescents from single parent homes

Living together and early marriage - Teens whose parents get divorced are more likely to live together, are more likely to marry as teens, and are more likely to marry someone whose parents are also divorced

Future divorce - If a child's parents get divorced, statistics show that it's more likely that their marriage will also end in divorce

- Could it be that the media and our popular culture have succeeded in convincing many of us that "divorce is no big deal", it's "OK", and that it "just happens?"

I mean after all, in the media we constantly hear about celebrities getting divorced on a regular basis. It's almost like husbands and wives are easily thrown away like facial tissue. A celebrity was recently married for 72 days. It's no wonder that so many people think that divorce is no big deal - sadly they think, "If I'm not happy with my husband or wife, if they don't treat me right, if I don't get what I want out of my marriage - I'll just get a divorce." When I hear someone say something like this, and I hear it on a regular basis from my students, it makes me think that many people really don't understand the amount of pain and heartbreak that divorce causes.* It makes me think that they don't understand that divorce throws millions of women and children into poverty. It makes me think that they don't understand the number one dream of many children is that their parents will get back together someday.

The truth is that divorce is similar to death except that divorce is the death of a relationship. Don't you think that it's unusual that many people think divorce isn't a big deal - but almost everyone thinks that death is a big deal? Over the years I've come to the conclusion that most of the people who think that divorce is "no big deal" haven't been through a divorce and they haven't seen the tears of children whose parents are getting divorced or who have divorced - unfortunately I've experienced the heartbreak of divorce firsthand and through my students - I've felt the pain and cried the tears of divorce and I've seen their pain and their tears - and I wouldn't wish it on anyone.

And please don't listen to the baloney that you may hear in the media about a "good divorce" - all divorces have negative effects upon people and their families. Tearing a family apart always does some damage.

I hope that I've made it clear that divorce can change the rest of your life for the worse.

Even though this chapter is about divorce - I think it's important for you to realize that a large number of people who are still married are unhappy. I just read some depressing information from a research study that followed couples for the first 13 years of their marriage. After 13 years, only about 43% of the couples were happily married - while about 21% of the couples were unhappily married, and about 36% of the couples were divorced.

Please take avoiding unhappiness in marriage and divorce seriously by using the information and suggestions in this book to make it more likely that you'll have a lifelong loving marriage.

*When I hear one of my students say something like, "If my husband/wife doesn't treat me right, I'll just divorce him/her", I worry that they'll end up being married several times - and when they're no longer young with good looks - that they'll end up having a miserable life.

Reflection: What negative effect has divorce had upon your immediate family, your extended family, or upon families that you know?

Sample marriage vow (promise): *"I, (name), take you, (name), to be my beloved wife/husband, to have and to hold you, to honor you, to treasure you, to be at your side in sorrow and in joy, in the good times, and in the bad, and to love and cherish you always. I promise you this from my heart, for all the days of my life."*

"Some people say that a lifelong marriage commitment is a nice thought, but reality is that keeping a marriage together for a lifetime in today's world usually isn't possible. If it usually isn't possible, then why do almost all marriage vows include phrases like 'until death do us part' or 'all the days of my life'?"

4

... PEERS HAVE TOO MUCH POWER

"Watch out for the negative power of peers"

So who do you think has the biggest influence on the behavior of many teens and young adults? You guessed it - peers. Many people are influenced by their peers to make bad choices of behavior in order to fit in. Unfortunately, these bad choices sometimes have long term negative consequences.

Let's try to understand why peers have more influence and are more important to many people than anyone. Could it be that we see and talk to peers every day? Could it be that we put more effort into developing our relationships with peers compared to anyone else? Could it be that peers give us positive and negative feedback about what we say and do every day? Could it be that peers are so powerful because we think that we need their approval and acceptance in order to feel good about ourselves and we tremendously fear their rejection? Could all of these things be reasons that many people have a closer relationship with their peers than anyone else?

Speaking of rejection from peers, I really understand why so many people fear it and desperately want to fit in because I used to feel the same way. Here's one example from my life: I ended up going to a new high school for my senior year because we moved. I didn't know anyone, they didn't know me, and my #1 concern was whether or not my peers would like me. I was so paranoid and so concerned about peers not liking me that I hardly said a word to anyone during the first two months of the school year. I was afraid that if I opened my mouth people wouldn't like me. Thankfully as the year went along I started to talk more and I made a few friends.

What I didn't realize at the time was that I was allowing peers to control my life. Are you or any of your peers making the same bad choice? A key turning point in the life of a person is when they decide to try to make a good choice in every situation regardless of what others say, do, or think. Caution: After you make this decision to try to make a good choice in every situation, don't expect an overnight change in regard to being overly concerned about whether or not your peers like you. It takes time to gradually become a stronger and stronger person. You'll know that you're making progress when you notice you're not so concerned about pleasing your peers as you used to be - especially weak peers who regularly make bad choices.

Over time you'll reach the point where you'll be in the habit of trying to make a good choice in every situation - regardless of what anyone else says, does, or thinks. Here's a suggestion for handling peer rejection: If a peer puts you down after you make what you thought was a good choice in a particular situation, don't worry or get yourself too worked up about it because that peer isn't a real friend anyway. Instead, do your best to ignore what the weak peer had to say - and then put in the effort to make more real friends by being a real friend (real friendship is discussed in the next chapter).

So what does all of this have to do with healthy relationships? Unfortunately, many people are under extreme pressure from their peers to date before they're ready. This peer pressure is both conscious and unconscious. Consciously, this pressure can take the form of teasing, putting you down because you don't have a boyfriend or girlfriend, questioning your sexual orientation, etc. Unconsciously, when a person sees other people with a boyfriend or a girlfriend, the natural tendency is to feel a bit inferior and to develop a desire to also have a boyfriend or girlfriend in order to fit in and feel good about themselves.

If you're strong and are able to resist the negative peer pressure to date before you're ready, it's more likely that you'll make good dating choices when you're ready for dating.

Reflection: How do peers influence your behavior positively and negatively on a daily basis?

"Since most people want to be liked and want to feel that they belong and fit in - resisting negative peer pressure is one of the biggest challenges that faces teens and young adults today."

"If you stop to be kind, you must swerve often from your path."
- Mary Webb

5

... WE NEED REAL FRIENDS

"Take the time to make and keep real friends"

You may be asking, "Why's having real friends so important?" The reason is that we're not meant to go through life alone. My suggestion is that you find a group of real friends to be a part of in your neighborhood, in school, in an organization, etc. Please be part of a group of friends who are interested in making good choices and having the best possible life. Sometimes it's hard to find this group and it often takes time to do so - but it's well worth the effort.

I had a tough time finding this group because I started school when I was 4 years old and up until 8th grade I was the youngest and shortest kid - and this made me an easy target for bullies and made some people not want to be my friend. The good news is that I eventually made a few real friends after I learned how to be a real friend.

Real friends will talk with you, encourage you, and help you through the downs of life. They'll celebrate with you during the ups of life, help you to stay focused on making good choices every day, help you resist negative peer pressure, give you wise counsel when needed (in other words, tell you what you need to hear even when you don't want to hear it) and hold you accountable for your actions. They'll truly be your friends for your entire life.

Just a word of warning about spending too much time with people who make bad choices regularly - you tend to become more like the people you hang with, so if you spend a lot of time with weak people, it's more likely that you'll mess up your life. Unfortunately as a school counselor I've seen this happen so many times - a good kid with good grades gets in with the wrong crowd and all of a sudden their behavior and school work goes downhill. And it's not just teens - a twenty something I know, who was raised right, started hanging out at bars with the wrong group of people. Now he's been in several bar fights and has been arrested twice for reckless driving as well as trying to get away from the police. (Please don't ever try to get away from the police under any circumstances - a 16 year-old who used to work for me as a counselor at a "Y" camp died when his "friend" decided to try to get away from the police after a traffic violation. He lost control of the car and hit a tree.)

Speaking of "friends", here's the true story about the first time I ever asked someone out on a date. I was a junior in high school, but I was only 15. I had my eye on a beautiful "blonde bombshell" that was a junior varsity cheerleader. I just missed the deadline for fall Driver's Education class so I wasn't going to be able to drive until the spring semester. I wanted to ask this girl out on a date, but I didn't want to have my Dad drive us and pick us up - I'd have been too embarrassed.

I told my "friend" Justin (name changed to protect the guilty) about my desire to ask her out on a date. He told me, "I'll drive you if you get a date, but you don't have the guts to ask her." Well, he was wrong. I practiced my asking for a date speech at least fifty times. I planned when and where in the school I would ask her for a date. I thought I had it planned perfectly because I was going to ask her to go to an away basketball game - games at which junior varsity cheerleaders didn't cheer. She didn't know me from Adam, but for some reason - I didn't think that was going to be a problem.

My heart was pounding, my mouth was dry, and the time had come. I walked up along side her in the hall near the end of the school day, turned to her and blurted out - "Hi, my name is Jim, I was wondering if you would consider going with me to the away basketball game?" She said, "I can't because I have to cheer." Awkwardly, I said, "I thought you didn't cheer at away games." She said kindly, "It's the only away game that we're going to this year - maybe some other time." I didn't know what to say so I just said, "Thanks." My knees were shaking as I walked away. It took me about an hour to completely calm down. That night I told Justin that I'd asked her for a date. His reaction was "What! - I never thought you'd do it!" I told him that I planned to ask her out again. He said, "Well if you do - I'm not driving you." That's when I knew he wasn't a real friend - he didn't keep his word.

I was so shy and embarrassed that even though I saw her in the hall periodically I never said another word to her. She probably thought that I was some kind of a jerk. Looking back, I now realize that it was a good thing I didn't start dating her - because I was nowhere near ready to be in a relationship.

A real friend:

- allows their friend to be themselves, really listens to their friend, and doesn't share what's been said

- can be trusted, supports and helps you, treats you with respect, sticks with you

- comes and talks with you as soon as possible when there's a problem in the friendship

- never encourages you to make a bad choice

- encourages you to make a good choice - even when weak people are encouraging you to make a bad choice

- tells you what you need to hear even though you don't want to hear it

- is willing to forgive you when you mess up

- understands that friendships change and can accept those changes after talking it out

(Years back as a substitute teacher a student told me that he and his "friends" smoked weed together regularly, that they were really close, and that they would pretty much do "anything" for each other. I listened and then politely said that from everything I've read smoking weed is even more dangerous than smoking cigarettes because it's been shown to cause cancer and it reduces how well your brain works. He said that all that stuff about the dangers of weed was made up by the government. A few weeks later the leader of the group was busted for marijuana distribution and the group of "friends", who would do "anything" for each other, scattered to the wind and no longer did anything together. They weren't real friends.)

Reflection: What can you do to have more real friends and/or strengthen your existing real friendships?

"A person's choice of friends is really important. Strong real friends lift you up. Weak fake friends pull you down."

"Friendships multiply joys and divide griefs."
- Henry George Bohn

"He's my friend that speaks well of me behind my back."
- Thomas Fuller

6

... WHY DATING IS SO IMPORTANT TO PEOPLE

"Humans do all kinds of things to try to feel good about themselves"

Have you noticed that people try to feel good about themselves in many different ways? For example: by being good at a sport, by winning a game, by rooting for a winning team, by playing a musical instrument well, by being a good person, by having lots of friends, by doing their best in school, by being great at their job, by buying as much stuff as possible, by using alcohol and other drugs, by being tougher and meaner than other people, by winning a fight, by gambling - the list goes on and on.

If you polled people about why they want to date you might get responses like: "I really like him", "I really like her", "he's exciting", "she's hot", "he's cute", "she's got a great personality", "most of my friends are in a relationship and I want to be like them", "I just want to have fun", among others.

I don't think that many people would come up with one of the main reasons if you asked them. I would like to suggest that one of the main reasons that most people want to date is that they want to feel good about themselves and/or they want to feel loved. After all it's only human nature - we want to feel important, we want to feel attractive to the opposite sex, we want to have someone who really cares about us, and we want to be respected by our peers. Being in a dating relationship usually helps us to feel good about ourselves.

May I suggest that our feeling good about ourselves isn't supposed to come from being in a dating relationship and it's not supposed to come from any of the other things that were

21

mentioned at the beginning of this chapter. A healthy way for a person to feel good about himself or herself is to be a strong person who tries to make a good choice in every situation. (A detailed explanation of what a strong person is and how to become one is in Chapter 9.)

Reflection: How important is dating to you and why? What makes you feel good about yourself?

"All of a sudden, I realized that being in the drama wasn't helping me. So I decided to ignore people who said mean things to me and to stop listening to people who were just trying to start drama. I pulled myself out of the drama and focused on having a few real friends and my schoolwork. It was a good choice."
- Anonymous student

7

... OUR CULTURE TEACHES US THAT EARLY DATING IS OK

"I really need a boyfriend - almost all of my friends have one"

Years ago my 6-year-old told me proudly, "I have 8 girlfriends." It was an innocent comment that sheds light on what our culture teaches us about dating. It teaches us that having a girlfriend or boyfriend before we're ready is "OK" or "cute." Obviously we learn it at an early age. You've probably heard a parent or a grandparent proudly say with a smile something like, "Kristen is 13 and she already has a boyfriend" or "Evan is 15, he's dating, in fact he's had 3 girlfriends already."

Unfortunately our culture doesn't emphasize the importance of people putting in the time and effort required to prepare themselves for a healthy relationship - and the result is that most people start to date before they're ready using the weak approach to dating. These people often get into an unhealthy pattern of becoming emotionally attached quickly to another person and then eventually tearing that attachment apart by breaking up when they don't "feel like" being attached anymore. This breakup often causes one or both people to go through the anguish of having their heart broken. If sex is part of the relationship, the breakup is even more painful - especially for the female. Sadly, many people don't learn from their bad choices and soon after their breakup they start the pattern all over again with someone else. They don't realize that being in this pattern damages their emotions.

People who have developed this pattern of behavior often continue it by eventually finding "the one", getting engaged, getting married, and when they don't "feel like" being married - getting divorced. Breaking the close emotional attachment of marriage is not that big of a deal for these people. Why? It's because they've broken an emotional attachment so many times before. Does that make sense?

Even after divorce a large number of people still don't learn from their bad choices and they repeat the same pattern again because they don't even know that they're in a pattern. Many celebrities have this problem.

Hopefully this book will help you to avoid getting into this unhealthy pattern or help you get out of it if you're already in it by using Strong Dating™ as explained in Chapter 15.

Reflection: Do you think that it's a good choice for a person to date before they put in the time and effort required to prepare themselves for a healthy relationship? Why or why not?

"If a large number of people are doing something (for example, speeding in their car, dating before they're ready, living together before marriage, etc.) - it's usually a sign that it's not a good choice."

8

... DATING BEFORE YOU'RE READY ALMOST ALWAYS IS A BAD CHOICE

"Raging hormones combined with dating before being ready is like driving around a sharp curve at ninety miles an hour with two front wheels that are about to fall off"

When a person starts to date before they're ready, the more likely they'll . . .

. . . date a weak person who regularly makes bad choices

. . . not do their best in school or at work (because they spend too much time with their boyfriend or girlfriend and not enough time working on homework, studying, or their job responsibilities)

. . . have sex before marriage

. . . contract one or more sexually transmitted diseases

. . . become a parent without being married

. . . marry before they're ready

. . . marry someone who's not ready to be married

. . . marry a weak person who regularly makes bad choices

. . . have an unhappy marriage

. . . be divorced in their lifetime

Over the years, people who made the choice to start dating with little or no preparation for a healthy relationship have told me things like, "I'm ready, I don't need to do anything to prepare", "I just want things to happen naturally and fall in love" and "I don't need any information/suggestions about dating because I want to make my own mistakes." Unfortunately, many of these people ended up messing up their lives because of their bad dating choices and because they didn't know the difference between having the feeling of being "in love" and true love (Chapter 16 explains the difference).

Reflection: Has dating before being ready had a negative effect upon you or upon someone you know?

"Dating, if done right, can possibly lead to the most wonderful experience that you'll ever have in life - a lifelong loving marriage"

"We have many choices every day. Some are more important than others. Be wise and choose carefully."

9

... HOW TO BECOME A STRONG PERSON

**"You're ready to date when you've become a strong person -
the type of person that you want to date"**

Last year when I was talking to a student who was having problems getting along with other students, I asked her to consider putting in the effort required to become a strong person. She seemed to laugh off my suggestion as something that wasn't very important. I think that the reasons she thought my request was somewhat funny were that she didn't really understand why I was asking her to consider becoming a strong person and that she didn't know what it means to be strong.

The reason I was asking her to become strong wasn't for me, it wasn't for her teachers, it wasn't for her parents, it wasn't for her friends - it was for her. Over the years I've learned that people who are strong are much more likely to be successful.

The Five Attributes of a Strong Person™ are:

- Character

- Attitude

- Responsibility

- Effort

- Self-control

Here are the attributes of a strong person in more detail:

Character (acronym = HIT)

- honesty - they don't lie, deceive, cheat or steal

- integrity - they do what they say they're going to do. In other words they're a person of their word. A strong person, who one day gets married, almost always keeps their marriage commitment to love, honor, and cherish their wife or husband for life. This means that they don't cheat on their wife or husband, they try to meet their wife's or husband's emotional, physical, social, and financial needs, and they try to love their wife or husband in thought, word, and actions every day.

- trustworthiness - they can be trusted in all situations

Attitude (acronym = CCFFHR)

- caring - they truly care about other people, they treat others in a caring manner

- cheerful - they try to be as cheerful as possible in all situations, they try to brighten the day of others

- friendly - they're willing to be a real friend to others including being willing to be a real friend to someone who's ignored or rejected by others

- forgiving - they're willing to forgive others who treat them with disrespect - even if the other person isn't sorry for what they've done

Many people I talk with aren't willing to consider forgiving someone who's treated them with disrespect - especially people who aren't sorry for what they've done and I can understand that. When I ask a student to consider forgiving another person, I usually also ask them if they think I'm trying to help the other person involved or if I'm trying to help them. They often say that I'm trying to help the other person. I say something like, "No, I'm trying to help you because when you refuse to forgive other people it doesn't help you because you're more likely to become an angry person - and an angry person is less likely to have the best possible life."

- helpful - they try to help others as much as possible because it's a good choice and because someday it's more than likely that they'll need help from someone

- respectful - they treat other people with respect, even people who don't treat them with respect and people who they don't like

Having a positive attitude is one of the keys to becoming a strong person. Remember that it's easy to have a positive attitude when things are going well. A strong person has a positive attitude even when things aren't going well. They're able to see the bright side of a bad situation. For example they might say something like, "Yeah, I'm not happy that I wrecked my car - but at least I didn't get seriously hurt.

Responsibility (acronym = HATS)

- for handling pains in a positive way (a pain is a person who you have trouble getting along with, who you don't like, and/or who has been mean to you)

I can almost hear you saying, "But I don't want to handle people who are pains in a positive way - I want to get them back for what they've done to me." I understand and I have to confess that sometimes I feel the same way - but I've seen over and over again that handling pains in a negative way just doesn't help a person in the long run. It doesn't help a person to be successful and to have the best possible life.

Handling pains in a positive way is a skill that you're going to need throughout your life because you're always going to have some people who are pains in your life whether it's at home, at school, or at work. It takes time to develop this skill - but with practice I've seen many people do it.

It seems to me that there are three types of pains. The first one is someone in authority over you (parent/guardian, teacher, boss, etc.) who's telling you what to do or is telling you something that you don't want to hear. A weak person has a negative reaction by ignoring what's said, by doing what's requested with a grumpy attitude, by refusing to do what's being requested and/or by being disrespectful. The problem with handling this type of pain in one of these ways is that it doesn't help you to have a positive relationship with your parent/guardian, teacher, boss, etc. Not having a good relationship with these people can create big problems for you.

The second type of pain is someone who's your peer or someone who you work with that you know isn't violent. These people can usually be handled in a positive and assertive manner. For example if this type of pain says something like, "Where'd you get that shirt?" in a negative way - you could look them right in the eye and say calmly and politely, "My guess is that you don't like it - that's OK" and walk away. If they keep giving you a hard time about the shirt, just say something like, "I think it looks good" in a positive way and then walk away.

Please keep in mind when you try to handle a pain you work with in a positive and assertive manner that it needs to be done delicately. (Once I was a manager and I had to fire someone from their job because they were constantly late. I fired her in a polite respectful manner. Much to my surprise, about six months later, she became my boss at another job and thankfully she treated me well. I think that part of the reason for this was the way that I had treated her when I fired her.)

The third time of pain is someone who you know is violent or someone who you don't know. As much as you feel like saying something negative or smart to this person after they give you a hard time, please don't do it. Please be strong and instead just completely ignore the person and walk away. (In other words, act like you didn't even hear them.) This suggestion could one day save you from being badly injured or killed.

You may have laughed at what I just wrote - but here are two true stories. #1: A high school student was walking home from school by herself and three guys were walking toward her on the sidewalk. As they passed each other the guys rudely stared at her and looked her over from head to toe without saying anything. She said with a negative tone, "What are you guys looking at?" An argument started and during the argument one of the guys picked up a small piece of concrete, came around behind her, and hit her in the head fracturing her skull. #2: A college student was talking on his cell phone close to midnight and a drunk guy came up to him and said in a rude tone, "Who are you talking to?" The college student said in a smart way, "Well, not you." Unfortunately, he was then beaten to death by the drunk guy and the drunk guy's friend.

A common thread runs through both of these stories. Neither of these people who were attacked realized that they were in danger and neither one was strong enough to handle these pains in a positive way by ignoring them. If they would've learned at a young age never to say anything to someone who's potentially violent or someone they don't know, these tragedies could have possibly been prevented.

If you still don't think that learning to handle pains in a positive way is very important, please consider this - one of the main reasons that people get fired from a job is that they can't get along with other people. And what's the reason they can't get along with other people? - that's right, it's because they never learned how to handle pains in a positive way.

- for always trying to make a good choice

I realize that this is very difficult because we're faced with so many choices on a daily basis. When people ask me, "How do I make a good choice when I'm under peer pressure to make a bad choice?" - I usually say, "Imagine that the person who loves you the most and who's strong (as defined in this chapter) is sitting on your shoulder whispering in your ear what the good choice is in a particular situation. If you do what you think they would tell you to do, almost always this will be a good choice." A person who remembers to do this when making choices will gradually make more and more good choices. They'll eventually become so strong that they'll almost always make good choices, they won't really care about what weak people say or think about their good choices, and they won't be too concerned if weak people don't like them because of their good choices.

A person who always tries to make a good choice is much more likely to have the best possible life than a person who doesn't.

Examples of good choices include:

- choosing to put in the effort on a daily basis to practice being a strong person

- choosing not to use alcohol or other drugs (Many of us don't think of alcohol as a drug because the media and our popular culture has glamorized how "fun" it is to use. However, it changes how the brain works just like other drugs. Because of their size, women are more likely to develop heart disease, cancer, and liver disease from drinking than men. Almost 1 out of every 5 teens who drink has a serious drinking problem. The earlier a person starts drinking, the more likely they'll become an alcoholic. About 1 out of every 10 adults who drink becomes an alcoholic. Binge drinking, more than 4 drinks for women and 5 drinks for men in one sitting, is increasing. As you read these depressing statistics, please don't think that everyone is drinking - 35 out of every 100 people don't drink at all.

- choosing to stay out of other people's business (Listening in and/or getting involved in other people's conversations, telling other people what you've heard (gossiping), spreading rumors, etc. - these things may be interesting and exciting in the short run because of the drama that's created, but they don't help you to have the best possible life because you develop a reputation as a person who's into other people's business.)

- for taking care of themselves

A teen who takes care of themselves sleeps between nine and ten hours (a young adult sleeps between seven and eight hours), eats a balanced diet including fruits, vegetables, breads, cereals, lean meat, and fish. They don't eat sweets and other "junk food" in large amounts. They eat a good breakfast every day, one that minimizes sugar - whether they feel like it or not - unless they have a medical condition that prevents this. (Breakfast is the most important meal of the day because it's been so long since the body has had food.) They have good personal hygiene. People who take care of themselves also don't do anything that would harm their body. Sadly the list of things that a person can do to harm their body is long. Many of these things are enjoyable for a short period of time, but they can cause permanent damage and some can even result in death. Regardless of what anyone else says or is encouraging you to do, choosing to harm your body is a bad choice.

- for serving others

May I suggest that the first group of people a strong person should serve is his or her family, relatives, and friends. He or she can serve them by offering to be of help whenever needed. A strong person also serves others by doing something that helps the community in which they live. Usually this involves some type of volunteer activity such as volunteering at an after school child care program, serving in a community service organization, joining a group that has adopted a highway by picking up litter on a monthly basis, offering to rake leaves or shovel snow for free for an elderly neighbor, etc. Serving others helps a person to get their focus off of themselves and on to other people (that's where the real joy is).

Effort

A strong person gives their best effort in everything they do. They're known as a hard worker. They believe that anything worth doing is worth doing to their best ability. They take pride in the fact that they always try to do their best even when their best isn't as good as someone else's best (because everyone has different levels of ability and skills - and that's OK). They know that giving their best effort will make it more likely that they'll have the best possible life.

More specifically, giving your best effort will:

- make it more likely that you'll do well in high school and get financial assistance and/or scholarship money to go to a trade or technical school, a two-year college, or a four-year college

- make it more likely that you'll do well in trade or technical school, a two-year college, or a four-year college and get a good job that you enjoy doing instead of a bad job that you don't like

- make it more likely that you'll do well in your job

A big part of effort is perseverance. Some people are only willing to give their best effort when what they're doing is easy and/or enjoyable. They often just give up when they don't feel like doing something and/or if it's difficult for them. A person with perseverance never gives up and keeps working hard even when they don't feel like it. If they get discouraged, it doesn't last - they quickly get back to work. They finish what they start.

Self-Control (acronym = BATM)

- of their <u>b</u>ody

Way too many people don't know how to control their body by only using violence when absolutely necessary for self-defense. Since movies, TV, video games, and other things in our popular culture make using our bodies to hurt other people seem OK and even exciting - many people don't understand how important it is to be strong by being a man or a woman of peace and that violence is evil. (What else can you say about something that killed a fifth grade student after she was hit with one punch by a sixth grader? When I say evil, I'm talking about violence itself - not the people who use violence. I may be naive, but I believe that some good can be found in everyone.)

A man or a woman of peace says or does nothing to start or to encourage a fight. They don't agree to fight anyone anywhere regardless of what names they are called by others. If someone asks them if they want to fight they said "no" and walk away. If someone attacks them for no reason they use self-defense (self-defense = using only enough force to be able to get away from the person and to get to a safe place).

My conversations with students who have a history of trying to solve their problems with violence often go something like this:

Student: "You've got to be ready to fight at any time in order to survive and to keep your reputation."

Me: "Hmm, when I look out the window I see lots of people outside who don't get into fights - how are they surviving?"

Student: "I dunno"

Me: "What eventually happens to people who try to use violence to solve their problems?"

Student: "They go to jail?"

Me: "Yes, a violent person eventually either breaks someone's head or worse and goes to the juvenile detention center/jail - or they get their head broken or worse."

Student: "Those things aren't going to happen to me."

Me: "How many times do you think that I've heard that?"

Student: "Lots of times."

Me: "Yes, hundreds of times."

I then bring out the front pages of the paper that I've saved about teenagers who were seriously injured or killed from violence and read the headlines to them.

Me: "So many of these people also thought - that's not going to happen to me."

Me: "Do you realize that all it takes for you to get hurt badly is for you to slip, to be off balance for a second, and then have the other person hit you just right?"

Me: "Do I have to visit you in the juvenile detention center/jail after you hurt someone badly or visit you in the hospital after someone hurts you badly and for us to share a cry for you to learn that violence doesn't solve problems?"

(I then usually tell the student the following true story about two boys who had the "That's not going to happen to me" attitude: "A few years back in a middle school where I was working two boys got into a fistfight after arguing about stolen lunch money. During the fight one boy fell and hit his head on the floor. Even though the EMT's arrived within five minutes, he still had to have emergency surgery that temporarily removed part of his skull to allow his brain to swell up without causing permanent brain damage - he came very close to dying because neither boy was able to control their body, anger or tongue. If this fight had happened outside of school, the boy probably would have died. So one boy almost died and other boy was sent to the juvenile detention center and now has a criminal record - all over a small amount of lunch money. I don't know, but I hope that they learned from their bad choices by changing their attitude about violence and by choosing to become men of peace. If this story didn't help the student change their thinking about violence, I usually tell them two other stories - one about a teen who's in prison for life sentence and the other about when I saw a person get shot to death.)

Me: "Will you consider becoming a man (or woman) of peace and not try to solve your problems with violence?"

Student: "I'll think about it." (some do decide to change)

A person also needs to control their body sexually. To be honest, I don't believe that there's such a thing as "safe sex" before marriage - and the reason that I don't believe it is because I've seen, heard about, and read about the damage sex before marriage does to people (explained in Chapter 15).

- of their anger

First of all, let me clear up a fairy tale that I hear from my students almost every day. They tell me that "so and so made me angry" and/or "I have an anger problem that I can't control." They don't seem to believe me at first when I explain to them that there's no such thing as someone else making them angry and that they can learn to control their anger if they really work at it. I try to prove this by showing them an example using my two hands facing each other, moving the fingers of each hand and making an angry "wa,wa,wa" voice back and forth between the two hands to simulate an argument between them and someone at home. Then I say that the phone rings and they calmly and politely answer it instead of yelling, "wa, wa, wa" into the phone. I then ask my students the question, "If other people make you angry and you can't control it, how in the world can you go from being angry one second to being calm talking into the phone the next? If it were true that you can't control your anger, you would answer the phone by yelling angrily into it." I also say, "Heaven forbid, but let's imagine that you've been in a car accident and you're lying in the hospital in a coma which means that you can't see and you can't hear because you're hurt so badly - and then a person who you say is 'making you angry' comes into the room and does the exact same thing that 'makes you angry' - would you have any reaction?" They say "no."

These examples help my students to understand that we hear things and we see things - and then we make a bad choice almost instantly in our minds to make ourselves angry. We turn our anger on just like a light switch - and we don't even realize it because we've flipped on the switch so many times before.

So how does a person control their anger? The first step is to understand that we make ourselves angry as just described. The next step is to realize that we all carry around an anger barrel (figuratively) with us. The anger barrel of some people has hardly anything in it, but the anger barrel of other people is near the top. When the anger barrel of a person reaches the top, the person either oozes (the person is grumpy, irritable, or depressed) or explodes (the person yells, curses, throws things, hits a wall, hits or kicks others, etc.). Sometimes people just ooze, sometimes people ooze and then explode, and sometimes people just explode. Different things make people fill up their anger barrel quickly - for some people it's an insult, for me it's when someone tells me something that I know is a lie.

It may sound like a ridiculous idea, but one way to control your anger is to imagine when another person says something mean to you, when they insult your family, when they roll their eyes at you, when they make fun of you, when they give you a dirty look, etc. - they're really just shooting an imaginary arrow at you. To make sure that you're not hurt by these arrows (and make yourself angry after the arrow hits you because they're painful), you need to put on your imaginary metal armor just like a knight as you get dressed every morning - so that when their arrows hit you, they just bounce off. They bounce off because you're *so* strong that you don't care about what weak people say, do, or think.

I ask my students how they would react if a 3-year-old said or did the exact same thing that their peer did who "made them angry." Almost all of them say that they would laugh it off and they wouldn't make themselves angry. I then explain to them that a weak person is acting just like a 3-year-old. I ask my students to stop, take a deep breath, and think "this person has a problem" when a weak person says or does something mean instead of making themselves angry - and then practice ignoring them or politely saying something assertive, positive, or humorous in a calm tone of voice. I realize that making yourself angry from what weak people say or do is a tough habit to break - but it can be done if you practice every day. (Please keep in mind that when you stop making yourself angry from what weak people say or do, don't be surprised if they get even meaner when you don't get angry. This is because some people actually enjoy trying to make you angry. To them, creating drama is entertainment. It's going to take a large amount of effort to constantly ignore them - but if you don't give in by being mean back to them, eventually weak people usually move on and find someone else who they can irritate.)

A key to controlling your anger is to find ways to drain it every day without hurting yourself or others.

People drain their anger in different ways, for example:

- taking deep slow breaths

- counting to whatever number you need to count to in order to cool off

- going for a walk around the block or around the office

- exercising

- listening to music

- pounding down on a pillow or a bed carefully with the side of your hands and a closed fist (thumbs up)

- going to their room to scream into a pillow

- going down to the basement to scream or yell (let people know what's going on so that they don't get scared) - some people find that it helps to also march in place while moving their arms and legs (like they're running) at the same time to release anger

- forgiving (as I mentioned before - not because the other

person is sorry or because the other person deserves forgiveness, but because it helps you to drain your anger barrel and it helps you not to become an angry person)

- of their tongue

The tongue may be the biggest thing that keeps people from becoming a strong person. I mean after all we live in a free society and we should be able to say almost anything we feel like saying - right? Well, the problem is that just because we have the right, doesn't mean that it's a good choice.

People who don't know how to control their tongue (use it wisely) are less likely to have healthy relationships. Billions of people have damaged or destroyed relationships with others, didn't get the job they wanted, or didn't get the promotion they wanted - because they said something without thinking first, spoke disrespectfully to someone or because they talked behind someone's back.

- of their money

You'll see in Chapter 24 that problems controlling money is one of the ten main causes of divorce. Many people have never been taught by their parents how to control money. They earn or are given money, but then it's spent quickly on stuff that they don't really need. It's very important that at least one marriage partner has the ability to earn what's needed to support the family and that both people know how to spend money wisely. I encourage you to read at least one book about how to control your money using a budget that includes saving for the future (a recommended book can be found on p. 118).

You may be saying to yourself - "Wow, becoming a strong person seems like a lot of work." It is, but it's worth the work because becoming a strong person makes it more likely that you'll have the best possible life.

So how do you become strong? First of all, you need to make becoming a strong person one of the main goals of your life. Only you can do this. Secondly, you have to develop the "I'm going to do whatever it takes" attitude toward achieving that goal. My suggestion is that you start by trying to be strong every day - in other words, you start practicing being strong. You start practicing having good character, having a positive attitude, fulfilling your responsibilities, giving your best effort, and displaying self-control. Please keep in mind that learning to be a strong person is just like learning a sport or learning to play an instrument - the more you practice, the better you get. At first it's going to be hard and you're still going to make some bad choices. That's OK, it takes awhile to break old weak habits like being mean back to someone who's been mean to you. Never give up. Some people find it helpful to start a journal where they write down what they did each day that was strong. Writing in a journal every day will help you to keep becoming a strong person as one of your main goals. Over time you'll be able to see the progress that you're making. (Some people find it very helpful to work together with a real friend toward the goal of becoming a strong person. You can hold each other accountable for words and actions and you can encourage each other to make good choices.)

My suggestion is that you don't even think about dating until you're sure that you're a strong person. If you're a female and someone asks you out, tell them, "Sorry, but I've decided not to date at this time." You'll probably be put down by people who are weak, but remember the goal is to become so strong that you don't care what they say, do, or think. If you're a male, forget about asking someone out until you're a strong person.

It takes real guts and lots of hard work to become stronger and stronger - but you can do it if you set your mind to it!

42

10

. . . IT'S VERY IMPORTANT TO ONLY DATE A STRONG PERSON

"Dating a person who's weak is like making the bad choice to hold a lit piece of dynamite and then hoping that it doesn't explode."

Not many people are interested in holding a stick of dynamite that's just been lit. But that's exactly what you're doing if you decide to date someone who's weak. It's just too easy to become emotionally attached to someone who's weak. No matter how nice they act towards you, how cute they are, how hot they are, how much money they have - please don't do it.

I know it sounds black and white and you might even be saying to yourself, "what could one date hurt?", but I need to warn you about the possible consequences. You need to realize that you're setting yourself up to become emotionally attached to someone that you shouldn't be emotionally attached to. You're setting yourself up for misery and heartbreak. Unfortunately I know - I made this bad choice.

Here's my painful story: I met a young lady at a fraternity party during my senior year of college. She was beautiful on the outside (the dangers of which are described in Chapter 13). We talked for about two hours, we seemed to have some things in common, and I ended up walking her back to her dorm. We dated for almost two years before we married.

After we got married it seemed like she was a completely different person than she was while we were dating. It was quite a shock to me because I didn't have any experience dealing with an angry unhappy person. Can you imagine having

43

things like a pot being thrown at you in a fit of rage?

After nine years of marriage she told me that she wanted to do "her own thing" and she moved out. On the day of the divorce hearing, just over ten years from when we were married, the judge asked her why she was seeking a divorce. She didn't have a reason. It wasn't until years later that I realized my two big mistakes - I dated a person who wasn't strong and I didn't carefully use dating to find out if the person I was dating had hidden serious problems.

(The good news is that I didn't make the same mistakes twice. Thankfully I now have a strong sweet wife of twenty-one years.)

Question: How come I'm attracted to "bad boys" - they're so exciting - and nice hard working guys seem so boring?

My opinion is that women are attracted to "bad boys" because they're somewhat wild, mysterious, and hard to tame. I also think that the media and our popular culture promotes that being a "bad boy" by being irresponsible, by treating women poorly, by moving from one dating relationship with sex to the next, and by breaking women's hearts is OK. Sadly, last year I read an article about a celebrity who said that she's looking for a "bad boy" who's ready to settle down. (Unfortunately she doesn't seem to realize that a "bad boy" is more likely to give her an STD, is much more likely to cheat on her than a strong person, and that taming a "bad boy" is a common female fantasy.) I believe that if you put in the effort to become a strong person you'll realize that having a relationship with a weak "bad boy" will almost surely mess up your life - and then they won't be so attractive anymore.

11

... THE STRONG LIFESTYLE IS ONE OF THE MOST EXCITING

"Being strong adds excitement and joy to your life"

Your reaction to the title of this chapter might be, "Yeah, right - being strong sounds boring and no fun."

Here's what living a strong lifestyle could do for you - it could help you to:

- have a good relationship with everyone in your family

- have real friends

- avoid depression when things aren't going well for you

- not waste your money

- find a strong person to date

- find a strong person to marry

- find a strong person to start a family with

- have a lifelong loving marriage

- get a good job that you enjoy doing after you finish your education

- be promoted to a better job

- have lots of good clean fun (including being goofy and silly, having a good laugh, and enjoying the company of others) without needing to be under the influence of alcohol or other drugs

Does all of that sound boring?

Here's a short story to give you a little example of how the strong lifestyle is one of the most exciting: When we lived in a small town in Virginia, the leader of an organization in our town accepted a new position in Chicago. The organization decided to give him a grand sendoff party - and grand it was. In the banquet room of Ernie's restaurant, one group after another from the organization performed a humorous skit or song honoring the leader. We almost couldn't stop laughing.

The presentation by 6 senior citizen ladies from the organization was the high point of the evening. The leader rode a big motorcycle for fun, so they dressed up in full length black leather motorcycle outfits and sang on stage the famous old motorcycle song "The Leader of the Pack." The laughter was almost deafening. At one point during the song, the leader stood on his chair waving his napkin in a big circle above his head with the music blaring to pump up the crowd. I noticed that the restaurant employees standing off to the side were wide-eyed and amazed about what was going on. Here was an organization, without any alcohol, almost raising the roof off the place. I think we did a great job that night of demonstrating in a small way that the strong lifestyle is one of the most exciting.

"It's not easy, but anyone can achieve the goal of becoming a strong person if they really work at it"

12

... EMOTIONAL MATURITY IS IMPORTANT

"Dating a person who doesn't have emotional maturity can lead to disaster"

In addition to what I've talked about in previous chapters, may I also suggest that you need to think about emotional maturity before you date someone.

Unfortunately, many people aren't emotionally mature enough to start dating (they, of course, will tell you that they are). Some people are emotionally needy - they need to be in a relationship with someone to help them feel good about themselves. They often are dependent and they don't know how to take care of themselves. In other words, they need to have someone take care of them. You need to be aware of the dangers of dating this type of person. They become emotionally attached very quickly and demand a lot of attention - they tend to suffocate you with their needs. Many people who aren't emotionally mature are selfish - everything is pretty much all about them. You don't want to date and marry a selfish person. Selfishness is discussed in more detail in Chapter 23.

In an ideal world, it would be great if people only got married if they were both strong and had a few years of work experience under their belts (after their education is finished). This is when it's more likely that people will have the emotional maturity needed to be married. It's almost like concrete - when you first graduate from high school, technical school, or college, and start a full-time job, the concrete for the foundation of your building (your life) has just been poured. Your identity, who you are as a person, is still in the process of being formed. It takes a few years for the concrete to fully harden, to be at its full strength. It's not good to join two buildings together (marriage) when one or both of the buildings have weak concrete. The possibility of collapse of the relationship (divorce) is much higher.

"You can't control what other people say and do, but you can control your reaction to what they say and do."

"See how a boy is with his sister and you can know how the man will be with your daughter."
- Oglala Lakota Sioux Indian proverb

13

... BEAUTY ON THE OUTSIDE CAN BE A TRAP

"Don't let beauty on the outside make you ignore ugliness on the inside"

The media and our popular culture are completely caught up in beauty on the outside (looks). Just page through magazines, watch TV, or go to the movies - they make it seem like looks is just about everything, like it's almost something to be worshipped. Unfortunately the media hardly ever mentions that many beautiful women and handsome men don't have the attributes of a strong person - which means that you should avoid dating them.

Men especially are attracted visually. When we get caught up in beauty on the outside, our brains tend to stop working. It's almost like we're a deer standing in the middle of the road dazed and confused staring at the bright headlights of a car coming toward us. The brightness of the person's beauty often causes us to ignore serious problems and danger signs because we're so mesmerized by their looks. Millions and millions of people have fallen into this trap - including me.

The key thing that we all need to remember is that beauty on the outside eventually fades with age, but beauty on the inside lasts for a lifetime. If you decide to get married one day it's a good choice to marry someone who's beautiful on the inside (a strong person). It's a joy to spend each day with such a person.

Please see the next chapter for information about how to recognize a person with beauty on the inside.

"Unfortunately a person who's beautiful or handsome on the outside is sometimes ugly on the inside - because their looks go to their head."

"A person with true beauty has the five attributes of character, attitude, responsibility, effort, and self-control."

14

... IT'S GOOD TO GET TO KNOW SOMEONE BEFORE YOU START DATING AND "THE CHECKLIST"

"Guard your heart by being careful about who you date"

Many couples start to date simply because they like each other, they think he's cute or she's hot - or as some of my female students tell me, they have feelings for a guy. Have you ever noticed how many people make important choices mainly based upon their feelings? Since I'm responsible as a school counselor for helping my students to be successful academically, personally, and socially - I usually ask them questions if they happen to mention that they're dating someone. These questions are designed to check if they're being as safe as possible with their body and whether or not they've made a good dating choice. After the safety question, I ask if it's OK to ask them some questions about their boyfriend or girlfriend. Most of them are fine with it. (If they aren't, I don't ask the questions.) My questions are something like, "I don't mean to sound nosey, but how well does the person who you're dating get along with their mother?", "How well do they get along with other members of their family and with their classmates at school?", "Does he or she treat everyone with kindness and respect?", "Does he or she think that school is very important?", "Is he or she a hard worker who gives their best effort in school?"

I've been surprised at the number of "no" or "sometimes" answers that I get when I ask these questions. When I get several of these answers, I have to politely ask something like, "I hope this doesn't sound rude, but if they can't get along with lots of other people and they don't do their best in school - why are you dating this person? Often their response is something like, "He's cute", "He's a bad boy and that's exciting", "She's hot" or "I love him." In other words, they're saying that even though their head says that it doesn't make any sense to date this person because the person isn't strong and that they'll probably end up with a broken heart or worse - they're going to listen to their heart (their feelings) and do it anyway. Choosing to date someone mainly because they're hot, you like them, or have feelings for them is a recipe for disaster. It may be hard to believe, but these things alone aren't good enough reasons to start dating anyone.

In order to save yourself from the pain and misery that usually results from a bad dating choice, please do whatever you can to find out if a person is strong before you even consider dating them. If you know they aren't strong - no matter what for your sake, please don't date them. Also, please don't date someone with the hope that someday you'll change them and they'll become strong - because people rarely change.

Here's how I got to know my future wife without dating: I met her in a young adult group. She and I were just acquaintances for about a year. During this time I was observing all of the ladies in the group to see how they related to other people. My goal was to get to know the ladies as much as possible without dating (I realize that this is easier for a man to do than it would be for a woman). I tried to participate in the group activities (retreats, football game parties, service projects, etc.) so that I would have a chance to observe their behavior outside of the regular group meetings.

My future wife showed me that she was a strong person by how well she got along with everyone. She had a positive attitude and she was friendly. I never heard her say an unkind word to anyone. She especially impressed me with the amount of time that she spent talking with a mentally disabled lady in the group. While most of the ladies ignored this person or tried to keep their conversations with her short, my future wife struck up a conversation with her on a regular basis, asked her questions, and seemed genuinely interested in her as a person. Her kindness to this lady really attracted me to my future wife.

"The Checklist"

When you're strong and you're emotionally mature enough to start dating, look for a person to date who:

- is strong

- has a good sense of humor

- has lots of things in common with you - recreational interests, hobbies, type and strength of religious belief (if any), values, lifestyle during childhood, etc.

- has a compatible personality to yours (Do you both tend to be introverted (shy, not very talkative) or extroverted (outgoing, talkative)?

- has integrity (They do what they say they're going to do. They're truthful with you and with others. They're honest with themselves - they can admit their bad choices and acknowledge their weaknesses.)

- always tries to make good choices - regardless of what others say, do, or think

- treats their family with respect, even members of the family who are hard to get along with (pains)

- treats all others with respect (even people he or she doesn't like or people who usually aren't treated with respect)

- is a hard worker (they give their best effort in school and/or at work)

- has a positive attitude almost all of the time

- is able to control their tongue (uses it wisely)

- has a healthy level of self-esteem (not too high and not too low)

- is a giving, caring, loving person

When you're ready to start dating, avoid dating a person who:

- isn't strong

- wants you to take care of them

- doesn't really want to grow up

- doesn't take responsibility for their actions (in other words, they think that almost everything that goes wrong is somebody else's fault)

- expresses their negative feelings (frustration, anger, etc.) in a destructive manner (yelling, swearing, putting others down, throwing things, etc.)

- is a controlling person

- you think that you need to change

- is a selfish person

Your reaction to this checklist may be something like, "How in the world am I going to find a person like that?" I agree that it's not going to be easy - but the first step toward finding a strong person is for you to put in the effort that's required to become a strong person as described in Chapter 9.

Question: What are the most important ingredients of a healthy relationship?

If I had to boil it all down to the four main ingredients that are needed in order to have a healthy dating relationship and possibly a lifelong loving marriage - I'd have to say: #1: both people being strong #2: both people having emotional maturity #3: having lots and lots of things in common with each other #4: chemistry. You can find out through dating whether or not both of you are strong people, whether or not both of you are emotionally mature, whether or not you have many things in common (your hobbies and interests, the type and strength of your religious belief (if any), your political viewpoint, your opinion about how children should be raised, your thoughts about how money should be spent, etc.) and whether or not you have good positive chemistry - the feeling that you really "click" with each other. Please use dating to be absolutely sure that all four of these main ingredients are there before you even think about the possibility of getting married. It's much easier to build a strong relationship using all of the ingredients than it is to repair an unhappy or broken marriage.

"Some people make bad dating choices using their emotions (feelings) alone - instead of first getting their emotions under control and then using them and their head to make good choices"

"Pretty much anything that's worthwhile takes time and effort - including developing and maintaining a positive healthy relationship"

15

. . . STRONG DATING

"Be yourself and use dating to gradually peel away their mask - find out what they're really like"

Let's say the time has come - you're a strong person and you're about to go out with someone who's strong. Here are suggestions for doing dating right:

Do:

- participate in a wide variety of wholesome activities together

- talk about a wide variety of subjects including ones that are controversial

- practice listening and also thinking before talking

- practice sharing your thoughts and feelings, both positive and negative, in a calm constructive manner - in other words, practice real communication

- talk through your disagreements (conflicts) and work them out in a calm manner

- accept and use constructive negative feedback from each other (for example if your significant other asks you to work on being on time for dates, work on it)

- try to find out if you have lots of things in common (having lots of things in common helps to hold a relationship together)

- find out if he or she has a set of real friends who are strong (If he or she's a loner, he or she may be looking for you to meet all of his or her needs - this can put a strain on any relationship)

- ask yourself the question: Is he or her selfish? Selfishness is a danger sign (please see Chapter 23).

- eventually ask him or her to gradually read this book and the book, *Fall in Love Stay in Love*, by Dr. Willard F. Harley, Jr. described in Chapter 19. Read the books yourself at the same time and then talk about them over a period of months (a good idea is to read a chapter at a time and then talk about it). Ask each other questions like: What were the most important points of the chapter to you?, What in the chapter didn't you agree with?, etc., What were your reflection question answers?

- after consulting with real friends and strong respected relatives asking them for wisdom and guidance, break off a relationship with someone who you know isn't the right person for you. Do it in a kind but firm way. Don't be sucked into the trap of going back into the relationship because now you're alone. Unfortunately many people stay in unhealthy relationships because their self-esteem depends upon being in a relationship. (Please see a professional counselor if you need to be in a relationship in order to feel good about yourself. Counseling often is available for little or no fee through health insurance.)

- break off a relationship in a kind and firm way with a person who's pressuring you to have sex before marriage (a strong person doesn't pressure their significant other into having sex - more about this later)

Observe:

- if he or she shows kindness and respect to all people - pay special attention to how he or she treats others who are often not well treated (people in low paying jobs, people with disabilities, etc.) Unfortunately, a person who treats others with disrespect is more likely to eventually treat you with disrespect

- if he or she's critical of others on a regular basis. This is a danger sign because more than likely they'll eventually become critical of you

- if he or she has a good sense of humor - including the ability to laugh at themselves

- if he or she becomes easily angered. This is a big danger sign because more than likely this anger will be eventually directed at you

- if he or she cares about other people and animals (does he or she have a tender heart?)

- how he or she reacts when something goes wrong and when he or she doesn't get their way or what they want - this will help you to get an idea of what his or her domestic personality is like. I read in a book, I think by the late O. Dean Martin, that we have a social personality and a domestic personality. The social personality is the one that we usually display in public - you know the cheerful and positive one. The domestic personality is the one that we display when we aren't out in public, our guards are down, and we aren't putting on our best face - it's more like the real us. It's the personality that you're going to have to live with on a daily basis if you eventually decide to get married.

After I was engaged to my first wife, she asked me if I would stay with her mother and her for several weeks while her father was out of town. A few weeks earlier they had an attempted break-in at their house and they didn't want to stay alone while he was away. She was asking me to drive a total of 3 hours every day to and from work. When I hesitated, she said in an angry tone, "Oh, I knew you wouldn't do it!" (I ended up doing it.) Unfortunately, I didn't realize it at the time, but she had just revealed some of her domestic personality

- how he or she treats his or her parents and other relatives (a lack of love and respect toward his or her family is a danger sign)

- how his or her father and mother relate to each other (Does one dominate the other? - a danger sign, Do they treat each other with respect? Do they seem to have a warm loving relationship? - often patterns in the parent's marriage are repeated when the child gets married)

- if he or she's too concerned with what weak people say, do, or think

- if he or she makes a good choice in situations when making a bad choice could personally benefit him or her - you're looking for a person who will try to make a good choice, no matter what, in all situations

- if he or she takes responsibility for their bad choices instead of making excuses

- if he or she apologizes for their bad choices

- if he or she forgives other people for their bad choices

- if he or she's a hard worker. Reality is that being a responsible adult requires a lot of work - both at work and at home. You don't want to marry someone who lies around on the couch while you do almost all of the work. A person who's a hard worker is more likely to be successful in life

Don't:

- put on an act and pretend to be someone you aren't just to make the person who you're dating like you (just as you're trying to find out what the person you're dating is really like, the person you're dating wants to get to know the real you - be yourself)

- let the thrill of someone treating you well and making you feel special cause you to ignore danger signs or serious problems - or to blind you from seeing that the person you're dating isn't strong after all

- let the fact that the person you're dating has money, or probably will earn a lot of money in the future, cause you to ignore their serious problems. Too many people have found out the hard way that the saying, "money doesn't buy happiness" is true

- ignore the danger of having the feeling of being "in love" with someone who you hardly know (infatuation) - a warning sign of being infatuated is that you spend too much time thinking about him or her

- become emotionally attached too quickly - take things nice and slow

- spend much time alone with him or her (especially if you haven't graduated from high school)

- be fooled that the excessive attention of a boyfriend or a girlfriend is true love - excessive attention is often something that people use to control others

- continue in a dating relationship with a boyfriend or girlfriend who has anger or addiction problems, who tries to control you (for example, tells you what to do or wear), is possessive or jealous, treats you with disrespect verbally or physically*, tries to keep you away from your real friends, or with whom the chemistry just isn't there

- rush into thinking about getting married - statistics show that longer dating relationships are more likely to become lifelong marriage relationships. My suggestion is that you use the Strong Dating™ approach for at least two years in order to really get to know your significant other - and that you wait until you're both at least 24 before you even think about getting married (Statistics show that the divorce rate drops significantly if you wait until you're at least 24. I know that sounds like a long, long time - but don't you want to maximize the possibly that you'll have a lifelong loving marriage?).

WARNING: please prepare yourself because the following five _Don't_ suggestions could be shocking . . .

- participate in make out sessions (affection is OK, but please consider eliminating make out sessions or at the very least keeping them short - for example 15 minutes - because long make out sessions can be harmful)

Even if you haven't torn the book in half, your reaction to this suggestion may be, "No one does that" or "That's absolutely crazy." I can understand your reaction - but please let me make a few points before you ignore this suggestion completely. So how can long make out sessions during dating be harmful?

- Long make out sessions often cause an emotional attachment to develop too quickly in a dating relationship. An emotional attachment can cause a person to not see serious problems in the person they're dating, to ignore danger signs, or to continue in a dating relationship that they know isn't right for them

- We get addicted to the feeling of arousal (caused by chemicals that are released in the brain) that we get when we kiss passionately. This addiction can cause a person to overlook serious problems in the person they're dating, to disregard danger signs, or to not recognize that the person doesn't have all of the attributes of a strong person

- If you participate in long make out sessions, over time they tend to gradually take up more and more of the time that you spend together as a couple - they waste important time that you should be using instead to really get to know the other person

- People who engage in long make out sessions during dating are much more likely to have sex before marriage because they lose control of their passions

- lay down together or turn the lights off - I know this may sound ridiculous and old-fashioned, but keeping your feet on the floor and keeping the lights on are good ideas to help prevent things from getting out of hand

- use alcohol or other drugs - their use is a bad choice to begin with and their use often leads to other bad choices

- tell him or her that you love him or her until you fully understand what true love is (please see Chapter 16)

- have sex with him or her before marriage

You may be saying to yourself, "What's the big deal about having sex before marriage? - everyone's doing it." First of all, the fact is that everyone isn't doing it. Just one example - according to a national survey, less than 50% of all high school students have had sex.

Secondly, it may be hard to believe if you've watched a large amount of garbage on TV and in the movies which shows that having sex before marriage almost never has consequences (it's possibly the worst, most damaging lie that the media spreads) - but having sex before marriage can be harmful to you and to your future. This harm could include:

- not feeling good about yourself

- finding out that having sex causes people to become emotionally attached way too quickly

- sex becoming the main focus of your relationship

- finding out that having sex makes people ignore danger signs and serious problems in the person they're dating - serious problems that could destroy a marriage

- failing to realize that dating relationships which have sex as their main focus usually don't last - until the relationship falls apart

- not learning to have real communication with each other, to be in touch with the your positive and negative feelings and the feelings of your significant other, to resolve conflicts in a calm constructive manner, to really get to know what your significant other is like in all situations because you're spending too much time having sex

- not feeling good about choosing to have sex after your

boyfriend or girlfriend says "I love you" and then later finding out he or she was lying to you just to get sex or he or she just has the feeling of being "in love" instead of true love

- feeling that you need to keep having sex with your boyfriend or girlfriend or else they'll break up with you - even though you don't feel good about it

- finding out that having sex makes people stay in dating relationships much longer than they should

- making the bad choice to stay in a relationship that you know isn't right for you because you're enjoying sex

- being broken hearted after your boyfriend or girlfriend breaks up with you

- becoming an angry person after having your heart broken

- becoming depressed or possibly even suicidal after having your heart broken (please see a professional counselor immediately if you feel depressed or suicidal)

- feeling that you can't trust anyone anymore after you've had your heart broken

- becoming more hesitant about eventually making a lifelong marriage commitment to another person after having your heart broken

- feeling horrible that you broke your boyfriend or girlfriend's heart when you broke up with them

- getting into the habit of jumping from one dating relationship with sex to another looking for true love and sadly never finding it

- getting a sexually transmitted disease

- getting pregnant

- becoming a single mother (guys often don't marry their pregnant girlfriends)

- having a child who doesn't have a stable male role model in their life

- ending up having problems relating sexually to your husband or wife in marriage because of the sex you had with them (and possibly with others) before marriage

- becoming divorced (statistics show that couples who have sex before marriage are more likely to get divorced than couples who don't have sex before marriage)

You may be saying to yourself, "How does this guy know about this damage - because my guess is that he didn't have sex before marriage?" You're right, but the reason I know this damage is real is because over the years I've worked with and I've heard about many people who made the choice to have sex before marriage and who damaged their lives.

You may be thinking, "This damage you're talking about isn't going to happen to me" - but that's what millions and millions of people thought before their life was damaged from this choice.

I realize that we live in a crazy messed up world where some people think that it's not a good thing to be a virgin - but if you are one, I want to encourage you to be strong and save yourself for marriage. It's going to be hard in today's sex saturated society, but *you can do it*. It's often helpful to be accountable to a real friend and help each other to remain strong.

If you've had sex in the past and you're not feeling too good about it, it's over, so forgive yourself, learn from the mistake(s), and make a strong commitment not to have sex again until marriage. If you're currently having sex - it's going to be very tough, but now is the time to stop and choose not to have sex again until marriage.** It may be difficult to understand, but if your boyfriend or girlfriend breaks up with you because you decide not to have sex with him or her anymore until marriage - they more than likely don't have true love for you in their heart as described in Chapter 16 and you shouldn't keep dating them. (A person who has true love for you does what's best for you and for your future together - not what they feel like doing.)

If you need help recovering from a broken heart or overcoming the need to be in a dating relationship with sex before marriage, I urge you to contact a professional counselor.

My hope is that you'll use the suggestions from this chapter to really get to know the person you're dating. Many divorced people feel that they rushed into marriage and they wish that they would have wisely used dating to get to know what their ex-husband or ex-wife was really like, including their domestic personality, before they decided to get married. It's true that using the Strong Dating™ approach isn't easy - but it's much easier than trying to fix an unhappy marriage.

*If you fear that the other person may become violent when you break off the dating relationship in a firm but kind manner, ask your parent/guardian for help and/or contact your local Domestic Violence Hotline or call the National Domestic Violence Hotline at 1–800–799–SAFE (7233).

**Unfortunately way too many women think that they have to give their body to their boyfriend in order to keep them. May I suggest in a kind way that this type of boyfriend isn't worth keeping because he's not strong. This type of boyfriend is more likely to break up with his girlfriend when he thinks she's not exciting anymore and research shows that this type of boyfriend is more likely to cheat on their girlfriend/wife in the future.

"If it's a good choice to have sex before marriage, then why doesn't hardly anyone who waited for marriage say they wish they hadn't waited? - and why do so many people who didn't wait eventually say they wish they would've waited?"

"To err is human; to forgive, divine"
- Alexander Pope

"A true test of character is whether or not a person respects everyone - even someone who most people think doesn't deserve respect"

16

... TRUE LOVE IS MUCH MORE THAN JUST HAVING THE FEELING OF BEING "IN LOVE"

"What the world needs now is love, true love."

Unfortunately, lots of people don't know what true love is and that's a big reason why a large number of marriage relationships are unhealthy and unhappy - and the divorce rate is so high. Many people think that true love is just a feeling. You know, having the wonderful head spinning feeling of being "in love."

If true love is just a feeling, feelings come and go. But true love doesn't come and go. True love is patient and kind. It isn't jealous, rude, selfish, controlling, or easily angered. It forgives. It's supportive, loyal, hopeful, and trusting.

Unlike having the feeling of being "in love", which is relatively easy to get especially during dating, true love usually develops slowly over a significant period of time (often years). True love is so much more than just having the feeling of being "in love" - it's supposed to be a lifelong commitment. When you say that you have true love for your significant other, may I suggest that you're saying you're committed to loving them for the rest of your life - for richer, for poorer, in sickness and in health, from this day forward, until death do you part. True love lasts - it almost never fails.*

Think of it this way, if a person has true love for another, it's like the sun - it's always there no matter what (remember that even at night, the sun is still there, it's just shining on the other side of the earth - and when it's cloudy outside the sun is also still there, it's just behind the clouds).

69

On the other hand, having the feeling of being "in love" is like sunshine - even though we'd like it to be sunny every day, the truth is that the amount of sunshine changes regularly. Some days it's nice and sunny and having the feeling of being "in love" is strong, on others it's partly cloudy and having the feeling of being "in love" is there but it's not very strong, and on other days it's cloudy and having the feeling of being "in love" is barely there at all. I'm hoping that this explanation is helping you to see that it's possible for a person to have true love for another person and not have a strong feeling of being "in love" with that person at a particular moment. (If you ask married couples if they always have a strong feeling of being "in love", I think they'll tell you that the strength of this feeling changes regularly.)

You may be asking yourself, "How can this guy talk about true love almost never failing when only about 6 of every 100 marriages last 50 years?" You may disagree, but based upon my experience, I think that one of the main reasons for this horrible statistic is that many couples marry when one or both people don't actually have true love for the other - many think they do - but actually they only have the feeling of being "in love" . . . and unfortunately just having the feeling of being "in love" isn't enough to keep a marriage going for a lifetime. When people who got married just because they had this feeling become unhappy in their marriage - often instead of going to professional counseling and putting in the effort to get back the feeling of being "in love", they just give up and get a divorce.

So when you hear someone say, "I don't love him or her anymore" - take it for what it usually is. It's usually someone saying that they've lost the feeling of being "in love", that they don't know how or they're not willing to make the effort required to get the feeling back, and that they probably never had true love for their significant other to begin with because true love almost never fails.

Many times I've heard young women say, "my boyfriend loves me." What they seem to be saying is that they think their boyfriend has true love for them. Unfortunately, most of these women have been fooled. How could their boyfriend possibly have true love for them if their boyfriend doesn't even know what true love is?

How would you feel if you gave something of very high value in exchange for something that you thought had a very high value - and you later found out that what you received was fake? Angry? Betrayed? Outraged? Depressed? How do you think that millions of unmarried young women feel after finding out that they've given their body to someone who doesn't have true love for them?

It's time for women to rise up and refuse to accept this fake true love from these men. Women need to realize that many men don't respect women - they see them as something to be used for their pleasure. I'm sorry if this sounds insulting - but it's time for many women to wake up, wise up, and not be fooled. It's time for women to become strong before trying to develop a healthy relationship with a strong man.

It's also time for men to stop treating women with disrespect and telling women that they "love" them in order to get what they want. In addition, it's time for men to become strong before trying to develop a healthy relationship with a strong woman.

*Please keep in mind that when I say true love almost never fails, I'm not saying that a person should always remain married to a person who emotionally and/or physically abuses them, who cheats on them, or who abandons them. Very sadly it's true that true love for another person can be destroyed by a husband's or a wife's words and actions. Please don't hesitate to contact a professional counselor if you're unhappy in your marriage or you fear that your marriage is in danger of failing.

Question: How can I tell if my significant other has true love for me?

This is a tough question because often it's difficult to tell if your significant other just has the feeling of being "in love" or has true love for you. Here are a few suggestions for telling the difference between the two: 1. True love usually doesn't develop quickly (crushes, infatuations, obsessions, and having the feeling of being "in love" develop quickly). 2. True love stands the test of time, it lasts. 3. True love has the qualities described earlier: patient, kind, forgiving, supportive, loyal, hopeful, and trusting - it's not jealous, rude, selfish, controlling, or easily angered. 4. A person who has true love for you is strong and wants to wait until marriage to have sex - because they know that it's a good choice and that it's the best thing for your future together.

"It's very hard for a person who doesn't know what true love is to find true love - because they don't know what they're looking for."

"Guard your heart - it's precious, so don't just give it away to anybody"

17

... THE DANGER OF HEARING AND/OR SAYING THE WORDS "I LOVE YOU"

"Only say these words to someone for whom you have true love."

I heard the words "I love you" about two months after I started dating my first wife. I didn't know it at the time, but my initial reaction was the right reaction. I said something like, "It's only been two months, you can't know that you love someone after two months."

But it didn't take long for my head to start swimming - in fact as I walked back to my dorm at college I jumped up in the air, pumped my first, and yelled softly, "Yes, she loves me!" Instead of seeing someone telling me that they loved me after two months as a danger sign, I was really happy and I absolutely believed that she had true love for me. I developed true love for her during the almost two years that we dated before marriage.

Painfully I found out the hard way, through how she treated me after marriage, that she only had the feeling of being "in love" when she decided to marry me instead of having true love. When she eventually lost that feeling and couldn't get it back even with many sessions of marriage counseling - she decided to move out and end what was supposed to be a lifelong loving marriage by divorcing me after ten years. I wasn't a perfect husband, but I had true love for her. I tried to demonstrate that love through my words and actions. I provided for her, I supported and encouraged her as she tried to earn a doctorate degree and I didn't deserve what I ended up getting - dumped.*

I realize it's hard for some people to not say "I love you too"

73

after someone says "I love you", but that's what needs to be done if you don't have true love for the other person. It's going to be awkward, but if you don't know what to say when this happens, you could possibly say something like, "thanks" and then try to change the subject.

So I beg you, before you say "I love you" - please be sure that you understand what true love is as explained in Chapter 16. Please don't say the words unless you really mean them - unless you're willing to make a lifelong commitment to the person who you're saying them to.

Also, please be suspicious of anyone who says those words to you who's been dating you for less than a year. Ask them what they mean when they say "I love you" and share what the words mean to you.

Please don't be completely fooled like I was.

*Sorry about my rant. I've forgiven her, but it still hurts.

"Have you noticed that in today's society the word love is way overused? We love our sports teams, our car, our favorite snack, you name it." The word love should be reserved for our significant other, our family, and maybe a few close friends."

18

... IT'S FINE TO BE SINGLE

"Married life isn't for everyone"

I can almost hear you saying, "What? Not get married? Are you kidding me?"

The fact is that it's perfectly fine to be single. Many people simply aren't ready to get married. Some people are more likely to be happy single and others are more likely to be happy married.

It's much, much better to be single than it is to be married to someone who you shouldn't be married to. Couples in millions and millions of unhappy marriages will sadly tell you that this is true.

A good number of people are somewhat desperate to "fall in love" and get married. These people often make a bad marriage choice because they don't take the time needed to really get to know the person they're dating before marriage, they decide to get married when they don't have true love for each other, and/or they don't go through a careful marriage decision making process such as the one described in Chapter 20.

If you want to get married someday - the best plan includes being patient, putting yourself in situations where you can get to know strong people without dating (by participating in activities of community organizations, service organizations, religious organizations, etc.) and working on becoming a stronger and stronger person every day.*

For many people, it's not easy to be patient, strong, and single - but it can be done. Strong friends can help you to keep being patient and will help you to keep trying to get stronger. Listen to them. Please don't give in and settle for dating a weak person who could mess up your life - just so that you can feel less lonely by being in a dating relationship.

*Please see p. 109 for a list of 21 tips that can help you to attract a strong person

<u>Reflection:</u> Can you imagine yourself staying single if you don't find a strong person to marry? Do you think that it's possible for a single person to live a happy fulfilling life? If not, why not? If so, how? Would you rather be married to a weak person than be single and lonely? Why or why not?

"If you put in the effort to become a strong person while you're single - you'll never regret it"

"Strong people are like magnets, they attract each other"

19

... KEEPING THE FEELING OF BEING "IN LOVE" TAKES A LOT OF EFFORT AFTER MARRIAGE

"Making the daily effort to keep the feeling of being 'in love' is definitely worth it"

When you have the feeling of being *so* "in love" while you're dating someone, making the effort to keep that feeling going doesn't seem very hard. In fact, most couples who have that strong feeling think it's always going to be that way without much effort.

It's quite a shock to these couples after marriage when they don't feel as "in love" as they once did (because everyone is somewhat of a pain to live with) and they realize how much effort is required to keep the feeling of being "in love" at a high level as much as possible.

I was reminded of the effort that's required to maintain this feeling when I watched the season finale of the reality show where people get voted off of an island. It was a close competition and a tie breaker of fire building was needed to decide who would be invited to the final tribal council. One contestant carefully nurtured the spark that he started with flint and steel, gradually blowing on it and adding small twigs until it became a roaring fire that burnt through the string to win the competition. Just like the contestant, both people in a marriage relationship need to make a daily effort to keep the fire of feeling "in love" burning.

Several authors have written excellent books on the subject of the importance of meeting the needs of your wife or husband and showing concern and respect for them through words and actions on a daily basis. My favorite, on the recommended book list on p. 118, is *Fall in Love Stay in Love* by Dr. Willard F. Harley, Jr. Please find a way to read this book - get it from the library, order it online, borrow it from a friend, do whatever's necessary (that's legal). It's 256 pages long, but it's filled with excellent information. The book clearly explains how to maintain a healthy relationship by keeping a high level of feeling "in love" as much as possible - and that keeping this feeling requires a lifelong effort. Following the suggestions of the book will help a couple to have the best possible marriage and to minimize the possibility of divorce.*

One of the best pieces of marital advice that I've ever received came from the best boss I ever had. He told me, "When I don't feel loving towards my wife, I try to do loving things for her and that makes me feel more loving." In other words, he changed his feelings by taking action.

<u>Reflection:</u> If you get married one day, what's your plan for keeping the feeling of being "in love" at a high level as much as possible in the marriage?

20

... HOW TO MAKE A GOOD MARRIAGE DECISION

"Important decisions need to be made very carefully"

I used to think that feeling "in love" and having true love for another person were good enough reasons to get married. I mean what else is there that's really important? Unfortunately I learned the hard way, through divorce, that these things alone aren't good enough reasons to get married and that these two things often cloud a person's thinking prior to marriage. Cloudy thinking (not thinking clearly) can make you rush into a marriage decision, blind you from seeing serious problems such as anger, addictions, selfishness, etc. in the person you're dating, cause you to ignore or minimize these problems, or cause you to pay no attention to danger signs.

Many people think that they're strong and ready for marriage - but they're not. On top of that, lots of people choose to get married way too quickly mainly based upon feelings without much thought. A quick choice is often a bad choice.

The decision of whether or not to marry someone is one of the most important decisions that you'll ever make. It's not a decision to be made carelessly or quickly. *Your happiness in life depends a lot upon whether or not you marry the right person.*

The following is a long list of hard questions, possibly unpleasant questions, which I suggest that you and your significant other think about as you go through the process of deciding whether or not to get married. Please take the time to ask yourself questions like:

- Has your significant other demonstrated, without a doubt, that they're a strong person? (Do they have good character, have a positive attitude, fulfill their responsibilities, give their best effort, and display self-control?) Are you a strong person?

- Do you think that you need to change your significant other or does your significant other think that they need to change you? (this is a danger sign because true love is unconditional and rarely do people actually change)

- Have you treated each other with a high level of concern and respect in both words and actions during your dating relationship?

- Have both of you consistently demonstrated respect for other people in words and actions during your dating relationship?

- Are both of you aware of your positive and negative feelings and able to express those feelings to each other in a calm constructive way?

- Do either of you ridicule the thoughts, feelings, and actions of the other?

- Are both of you able to control your tongue? (please see Chapter 21) Do either of you like to complain?

- Do you listen well to each other? Are you both able to sense the feelings behind each other's words?

- Do both of you have good communication and conflict resolution skills?

- Have you had experience resolving conflicts together and expressing negative thoughts as well as feelings in a constructive way during your dating relationship? (For example, did you express your negative thoughts and feelings in a calm manner when your significant other took a phone call or was distracted by the TV - in the middle of an important conversation with you?)

- Have you communicated well during your dating relationship?

- Have both of you completed your education and have at least two years of work experience under your belts? Have both of you taken care of yourself alone for at least a year? - in other words, do you both know how to cook, clean, wash clothes, control money, etc.?

- Do you or your significant other have addictions - alcohol or other drugs, pornography, gambling, etc.?

- Are either of you too selfish to be married? Marriage requires putting the other person first most of the time - which is a shock to many people (please see Chapter 23)

- Do both of you have the same definition of true love?

- Do you have true love for each other or does one or both of you just "love feeling loved?"

- Do you have true love for each other or does one or both of you just want the other person's body?

- Are you "in love" with the lifestyle that your significant other can provide for you after marriage (remember that money can't buy happiness)? Is your significant other "in love" with the lifestyle that you can provide for him or her after marriage?

- Are you "in love" with who your significant other could

become (for example, a person with an important job) instead of who they are now or is your significant other "in love" with who you could become instead of who you are now?

- Are you or your significant other trying to get away from parents/guardians by getting married?

- Are you trying to get your significant other out of a bad situation or get yourself out of a bad situation through marriage?

- Has your significant other tried to control you while dating by telling you what to do, what to wear, or by keeping you away from your friends? Have you tried to control your significant other?

- Does your significant other treat you like a child or do you treat your significant other like a child?

- Are you or your significant other weak and have the desire to be taken care of through marriage? (Sorry if the last several questions sounded especially insulting, but marriage is supposed to be an interdependent relationship between two strong people - not a relationship with one person who's completely dependent upon the other or with one person who dominates or controls the other.)

- In addition to having true love for each other, do both of you have the feeling of being "in love?" In other words, do you have strong romantic feelings for each other? Is the chemistry there - do you really "click" with each other? Do other people notice and comment about the chemistry they see between the two of you?

- Does one or both of you have an unrealistic view of what marriage is going to be like? Do both of you have the same expectations for marriage? (Some people believe that everything is going to perfect after marriage - instead of realizing that marriage has its ups and downs and that keeping the feeling of being "in love" at a high level as much as possible takes a lot of effort.)

- Are your personalities fully compatible? (They say that opposites such as introverts and extroverts sometimes attract, but people with similar personalities are more likely to stay together in marriage for a lifetime.)

- Do you both agree to do whatever it takes to avoid divorce and that divorce will not even be an option if you decide to get married?

- Have you both read this book and the book *Fall in Love Stay in Love* by Dr. Willard F. Harley, Jr. cover to cover?

- Based upon the principles in Dr. Harley's book, after you're married:

  - are both of you willing and able to communicate your needs to each other on a daily basis?
  - are both of you committed to doing your best to meet the needs of each other on a daily basis?
  - are both of you willing to make the effort required to treat your wife or husband consistently with concern and respect in thoughts, words, and actions?
  - are both of you willing to make the effort required to keep the feeling of being "in love" at a high level?

- Do you have lots and lots of things in common? (recreational interests, hobbies, type and strength of religious belief (if any), opinion about how money should be spent, thoughts about how children should be disciplined, values, the lifestyle in which you and your significant other were raised, political views, etc.)

- Are you in agreement about what's important to you? - for example: having a clean picked up house, eating a healthy balanced diet, exercising on a regular basis, having close relationships with friends and/or family, living as close as possible to family, etc.

- Have you had a chance to observe your significant other's behavior when things go wrong as well as when making a good choice is hard? Has your significant other had an opportunity to observe your behavior when things go wrong as well as when making a good choice is hard?

- Have you allowed your significant other to see the real you during your dating relationship instead of putting on an act? Has your significant other allowed you to see the real him or her or have they just been putting on an act during your dating relationship?

- Do both of you have the attitude of a strong person almost all of the time (caring, cheerful, friendly, forgiving, helpful, and respectful)? A husband or wife who has a weak negative critical attitude will make your life miserable.

- Have both of you shown the ability to admit mistakes/ask for forgiveness and the willingness to forgive each other? (people in a marriage relationship need to be able to admit mistakes/ask for forgiveness and forgive each other on a daily basis)

- Are you or your significant other ignoring or minimizing

any serious problems or danger signs because one or both of you really want to get married?

- Do both of you want children? If you have children, do you agree on how the children should be raised? (whether or not they'll be placed in day care, how they should be disciplined, how much stuff they should be given, whether they should be required to do chores, religious training (if any), etc.)

- Are you and/or your significant other able to earn what's needed to support a family? Are both of you willing and able to control your spending in order to remain within a budget? Will you and your significant other be satisfied with the lifestyle that you can afford on this budget?

- A person who does premarital counseling told me that it's important for people considering marriage to have similar life purposes. He suggested that couples ask themselves questions like: Do we want similar things out of life?, Do we have similar goals and dreams?

- Are both of you hard workers - but not workaholics? (Workaholics often neglect their personal life.)

- Are both of you at least 24 years of age? (as I mentioned before, statistics show that the divorce rate for people who marry at age 24 or above is significantly lower than those who marry below age 24)

- Do you both agree that you'll immediately seek professional marriage counseling if one or both of you are unhappy in the marriage?

- Have you attended in-depth premarital counseling with

a professional counselor that includes communication and conflict resolution training?

Whew! - as you can see there are many questions that need to be carefully considered as you go through the process of deciding whether or not to get married. It's also a very good idea to seek the counsel of relatives and friends who are strong. If the majority of relatives and friends who are strong are opposed to your getting married - it's almost always best to decide not to get married, or at the very least postpone the decision. There's no reason to rush into what could be a bad decision. If he or she's unhappy that you need more time to decide, it could be a danger sign because true love is patient.

Someday in your life it's probable that you'll be faced with a marriage decision. This chapter was written to help you make a good decision - a decision that will minimize the possibility of divorce and maximize the possibility that you'll have a lifelong loving marriage.

"If you get engaged one day, continue to use the engagement time to find out what your significant other is really like - just like you did while you were dating. The stress of all the planning and preparation that takes place during engagement often helps to reveal what your future spouse is really like. If you see a serious problem or a danger sign during engagement, please don't just ignore it - be strong and immediately get professional counseling. The outcome of counseling may be to continue on with the wedding as planned, to postpone it, or to cancel it. A broken engagement is much better than a broken marriage."

21

... AN UNCONTROLLED TONGUE ISN'T A GOOD THING

**"It's very hard for many people to get their tongue
under control by thinking before talking"**

I messed up yesterday. I talked to my wife in a way that wasn't kind. Instead of treating her like an adult and expressing my negative thoughts and feelings in a calm constructive manner about a particular situation, I talked to her like she was the child and I was the parent - not a good way to treat her with respect and to make her feel loved. Thankfully, we were able to talk it out and I told her that I was sorry for expressing my thoughts and feelings in a negative destructive way.

The reason I brought this up is to give you an example that, even after many years of marriage*, I'm still making bad choices using my tongue. Unfortunately it's a daily battle that sometimes the tongue wins. The uncontrolled tongue does a huge amount of damage to both dating and marriage relationships. Think about all of the thoughtless and uncaring words that are spoken between husbands and wives - words that would never be said, especially in the way that they're often said, if people were keeping their marriage vow (their promise) to love, honor, and cherish their wife or husband.

At this point in his life, my teenage son thinks that he should say what's on his mind when it's on his mind. He thinks that holding things in isn't good for him - you know, like he might develop stomach problems. We've tried to explain to him that sometimes things need to left unsaid or at the very least not be said until everyone has had a chance to cool off and a calm conversation can take place. We've tried to teach our children to ask themselves questions in their minds before saying something. Questions like: 1. Am I calm? 2. Is the other person calm? 3. Does it need to be said? 4. Will saying it make the situation better? 5. Is it a good choice to say it? 6. How can I say what needs to be said in a way that's as positive as possible? 7. Is this the right time and place to say it?

This chapter was included because many people don't realize how important it is to use their tongue wisely and how much damage an uncontrolled tongue can cause to a relationship. You may be forgiven after you say something without thinking, but sometimes it takes a long time for the damage to be repaired. (This is because people have a tendency to remember what you said thoughtlessly and replay it in their minds. Their trust that you will not try to hurt them with your words has been temporarily broken.) I encourage you to practice along with me thinking before talking and controlling the tongue. Learning how to use it in a positive manner will help you to build healthy relationships in all areas of your life.

*Unfortunately the tongue seems to get more out of control when we move from dating (an uncommitted relationship in which either person could leave at any time) to marriage (a committed relationship in which either person could leave at any time but not without breaking their marriage vows and usually costing thousands of dollars in legal fees for a divorce and possibly alimony). Over the years I've been shocked and saddened to hear how some married couples talk to each other.

"Wisdom is divided into two parts: 1) having a great deal to say 2) not saying it
- Anonymous

"Before you say what you think - think"
- Anonymous

22

... ABOUT THREE DANGEROUS ATTITUDES

**"We love each other so much, it'll always be this way,
we'll never get divorced."**

As I mentioned before, I used to have the "divorce won't happen to me" attitude. Never in my wildest dreams did I ever imagine being divorced. After all, I came from a good family with parents committed to each other, I was a nice person, I tried to meet her needs, and I thought we had true love for each other. Even when things got rough and we were in professional marriage counseling, I told myself that everything was going to be all right because we loved each other.

Unfortunately, my first marriage still ended in divorce because at the time of our marriage both of us were not as strong as we needed to be and she just had the feeling of being "in love." (Looking back, I also realize that we didn't put enough effort into keeping the feeling of being "in love" at a high level as described in Chapter 19.)

The truth is that the "divorce won't happen to me" attitude is dangerous because it can cause you to make a bad choice of a marriage partner and after marriage it can cause you to think that you don't need to put much effort into keeping the feeling of being "in love." A lifelong loving marriage takes two people deeply committed to each other, a willingness to grow up (ouch) - as well as a lot of hard work, love, and forgiveness.

Another dangerous attitude is "divorce is no big deal." Please don't let seeing celebrities go through one divorce after another fool you into thinking that divorce is no big deal. As I stressed in Chapter 3, it's a big deal for almost everyone who gets divorced.

The reason why the "divorce is no big deal" attitude is so dangerous is that people with this attitude are less likely to carefully go through the marriage decision making process described in Chapter 20 and are more likely to make a bad choice of a marriage partner. They are also more likely to give up on their marriage if they are unhappy.

And finally, the "I know it all" attitude is dangerous. Have you ever noticed that regardless of our age many of us, including myself, at times seem to think we "know it all?" Sadly, I've seen this attitude in some teens and young adults that I've talked with over the years - you probably have to. The truth is that none of us "know it all" and that life is supposed to be a lifelong learning and growing process.

The danger is that people with this attitude tend to stop learning and stop trying to become a stronger and stronger person. Because of this, they often learn their lessons the hard way by making bad choices in regard to dating and marriage.

My hope is that this book will help you to not have any of these three attitudes and to make good choices in regard to dating and marriage.

Reflection: Do you have any of these three attitudes? If so, what can you do to change these attitudes?

23

... SELFISHNESS DAMAGES RELATIONSHIPS

**"Contrary to what many people think, the best possible
life isn't found in personal gain and personal pleasure
(selfishness) - it's found in caring about and loving others."**

As a teen and a young adult, I never heard anyone talk about
the two main values in our society. If they did, I wasn't paying
attention.

I'm not sure where, but I heard or read somewhere that the two
main values in our society are personal gain and personal
pleasure. Think about it, aren't they the main two things that
most people are concerned about? - people want to get as much
as they can (money, stuff, etc.) and they want as much pleasure
as possible (alcohol and other drug use, sex outside of
marriage, gambling, you name it). Unfortunately, many people
have been brainwashed by the media and by their "friends" into
thinking that personal gain and personal pleasure - in other
words selfishness - is the way to happiness. Many people think
that if something's exciting or feels good, do it.

We're naturally selfish - we're concerned about having food we
like, good clothes, a nice place to live, all kinds of stuff, as well
as lots of fun. Face it, we live in a "Me First" society - many
people want what they want when they want it. However, too
much selfishness can be destructive to yourself and to your
relationships with others. It may not seem to make any sense,
but forgetting about yourself and focusing on caring about and
loving others is a good way to find happiness.

Here's a quick example of what I'm trying to communicate:
Before my wife and I had children we went to amusement parks

and rode all of the fast thrill rides from opening to closing. After we had children, my main source of joy was no longer from the excitement of riding the rides that I wanted to ride (selfishness) - instead it was from seeing the joy on their faces as they had fun riding the rides that they wanted to ride. My focus was off of myself. My joy came from loving them by going on their favorite rides (and at 6'6" tall I didn't fit very well into the little train). It may be hard to believe, but I got just as much enjoyment sitting in the shade watching them go around in circles on the little kiddie airplanes as I did when I was going on the fastest scariest ride.

If you decide one day to get married, it's important to realize that a big problem that you're going to have to battle on a daily basis is selfishness. You go through most of your single life with yourself as your #1 concern. If you get married, all of a sudden after a few words said by a person who has a license to perform marriages, someone else that you love is supposed to be your #1 concern. You're now #2. (If you have children, you become an even lower priority.) When you get married - you make a promise to love, honor, and cherish your lifelong mate regardless of whether you feel like doing it and regardless of what you receive in return. It's supposed to be an unconditional promise. (Not an "I'll give you this if you give me that" promise.)

To many people who get married, having to put someone else first is a big shock - it means that they can no longer say or do whatever they want whenever they want. It takes awhile for some people to adjust to this new reality because old habits are often slow to die. I have to confess that there are times when I'm not happy about having to put my wife first and sometimes I fail to put her first. I have to try each day to be less selfish and to do a better job of loving my wife and family.

I realize that it's hard for some people to understand that being selfish will not help them to have the best possible life. Let me explain it in another way - too much selfishness is like eating too much candy. If you keep eating too much candy, you'll eventually end up overweight or sick. Too much selfishness gradually damages your relationships with others. Quite frankly, they get sick of your selfishness.

An idea for teens:

I came up with a somewhat silly but fun way to help people in our family to recognize selfishness - when someone says something that's just out and out selfish, for example bragging about how great they are, the other people together say "goy!" in a funny way. Goy! stands for "**g**et **o**ff **y**ourself." When someone is demanding their own way, we give them a "goy!" Usually everyone starts laughing after it's said. Talk this idea over with your family and see if they want to try it.

I've also seen real friends use this idea to successfully help each other be less selfish.

"A person who is loving, caring, and giving - and who tries to put the needs of others first by getting off of themselves, is more likely to have the best possible life."

"Selfishness is the greatest curse of the human race."
- **William E. Gladstone**

"It's true that a selfish person may be happy for a short period of time, but I've never met a selfish person who's been happy, content, and fulfilled throughout their entire life."

"Selfishness is like a drought - it makes relationships wither."

"Have you noticed that people who have the selfish 'do whatever feels good whenever you feel like doing it' attitude almost always eventually mess up their lives?"

24

. . . THE TEN MAIN CAUSES OF DIVORCE

"True love lasts - it almost never fails"

Over the years I've compiled the following list of what in my opinion are the main causes of divorce (in no particular order)*:

1. The husband and/or the wife did not put in the time and effort required to become strong before dating and marriage - and because of this, one or both of them are not as strong as they need to be

2. One or both people not having true love for the other, not knowing what true love is, or possibly not understanding that even happily married couples don't have the strong feeling of being "in love" all the time. (Many couples don't realize that emotions are heightened while dating because they're in an uncommitted insecure relationship - everything seems extremely exciting and intense. They misinterpret the natural reduction of emotions that takes place in marriage, a committed secure relationship, as "we don't love each other the way we used to" or "we're not 'in love' anymore.")

3. Selfishness - which is often displayed through a "Me First" attitude. People who are selfish often seek a divorce because they're not getting what they want from their wife or husband (affection, attention, possessions, lifestyle, excitement, respect, etc.). They don't understand that when they got married they made a promise that they would love their wife or husband regardless of what they receive back from them (ideally this promise is only supposed to be broken in situations of abuse, abandonment, or cheating after intensive marriage counseling)

4. Too high of expectations - many couples expect to have the strong "we're *so* in love" feeling they had before marriage to continue throughout marriage without much effort. They expect their wife or husband to meet all of their needs. They truly believe the fantasy that they'll "live happily ever after" without problems. When they have conflicts, which are going to happen in any relationship, they possibly even start thinking, "we don't love each other anymore." Reality is that any marriage relationship is going to have ups and downs

5. Unwillingness of one or both people to make the effort required on a daily basis to keep the feeling of being "in love" at a high level by trying to meet the needs of their wife or husband and by treating each other with concern and respect. A person who does premarital counseling told me that it's amazing the amount of effort that couples are willing to put into a relationship before marriage and how little effort they're willing to put into a relationship after marriage. He said that relationships are like grass - they need watering (quality time together, date nights, etc.) to stay green and healthy. Keeping a healthy relationship strong takes work and maintenance

6. Emotional and/or physical abuse and/or cheating

7. Power Struggles - these occur when one or both people in the marriage selfishly try to dominate or control the other in order to have their own way (husbands and wives are supposed to treat each other with mutual love and respect)

8. Poor Communication and Conflict Resolution Skills - many people don't know how to communicate well and how to resolve conflicts in a calm constructive way that doesn't damage the relationship**

9. One or both people being unable or unwilling to control money

10. One or both people aren't emotionally mature enough to be married and aren't willing to put in the effort to grow up

*Of course, divorce often occurs from a mixture of these causes.

**Research shows that the use of electronics to communicate is becoming an obsession for many teens and young adults (some people have a panic attack if they don't have their electronic device of choice with them). Research also shows that this obsessive use is causing a reduction in face-to-face communication skills. These skills are needed by everyone in order to communicate well throughout their lives. Both people in a conversation need to be able to see each other in order to fully understand the words and feelings that are trying to be communicated because 75% of face-to-face communication is nonverbal and only 25% is verbal. The only way for a person to develop their face-to-face communication skills is to practice talking with others face-to-face. So how does a person force themselves to practice? A suggestion is that they consider turning electronics off completely during a specific time of the day (and let their friends and relatives know that they're doing it) - and then find someone to have an uninterrupted face-to-face conversation with during that time.

Question: Is living together a good choice?

The number of unmarried couples living together has skyrocketed during the past few decades. Many of these couples think that living together isn't a problem because "pretty much everyone is doing it." It's now unusual to attend a wedding of a couple who hasn't lived together.

I've heard lots of reasons why people live together including, "He's not ready to make a commitment", "We want to be sure that we're compatible", "Two can live almost as cheaply as one, it's helping us to save up for a house", "We want to work for a few years before we get married", "We're going to get married eventually, we're just not sure when", etc.

My opinion is that living together is a bad choice - no matter how many people are doing it. Most research shows that couples who live together before marriage are more likely to:

- get divorced than couples who don't

- be unhappy in their marriage than couples who don't

- cheat on their wife/husband than couples who don't

If your significant other wants to live with you before marriage, it's a sign that he or she may not be a strong person because a strong person always tries to make a good choice, a choice that's the best thing for the relationship in the long run - and this includes the hard choice of deciding not to live together.

"People who use living together as a test drive before marriage are much more likely to have a major wreck after marriage - divorce."

EPILOGUE

"A cultural revolution is needed"

In my opinion, we need a cultural revolution in order to help significantly reduce the divorce rate in our society that has become a pandemic. The proposed revolution may sound extreme - but I'm suggesting that people consider waiting until they're a strong person and are at least a freshman in high school before trying to find a strong boyfriend or a strong girlfriend. In other words, I'm suggesting that people don't date until they have good character, have a positive attitude, fulfill their responsibilities, give their best effort, and have self-control. I'm also suggesting that teens who are strong consider only group dating until they're a junior or senior in high school (if they choose to date at all). *Unfortunately, the pandemic of divorce needs strong medicine.*

I can almost hear the younger teens reading this book screaming things like: "That doesn't make any sense, what are we going to do for fun? What are we going to do on the weekends? That would make life so boring. All the good ones will be gone by then!" And I can hear the parents and grandparents screaming: "I married my high school sweetheart and it turned out just fine. I dated at an early age and I'm going to let my child/grandchild do the same. Don't suggest that my child/grandchild should wait to date one-on-one until they're a junior or senior in high school - I think that's too long to wait!"

Before you get yourself too worked up, here's what the cultural revolution would look like when it's achieved -

A dramatic increase in the number of:

- people who are strong

- people waiting until they're strong before they date

- strong people who will only date other strong people

- teens who are participating in one-on-one dating and group dating using the Strong Dating™ approach to dating

- young adults who are participating in one-on-one dating using the Strong Dating™ approach to dating

- wholesome and fun recreational activities available for teens and young adults on Friday and Saturday nights at a reasonable cost

- people who are in healthy dating relationships

- people in lifelong loving marriage relationships

- people who are having the best possible life

A dramatic decrease in the:

- number of people who are dating without being strong

- number of people who are dating a weak person

- number of people who are participating in one-on-one dating and group dating using the weak approach to dating

- the number of people with sexually transmitted diseases (The current numbers are absolutely shocking - a national study by a government agency showed that at least 1 out of every 4 (25%) of teenage girls has an STD.

Sexually active people don't seem to realize or don't seem to care that they're taking a high risk of damaging their health. Many people mistakenly think "It's not going to happen to me.")

- amount of pain and anguish caused by broken hearts (The amount of pain and anguish caused from broken hearts in our society is incredible and sad. Please be a real friend and suggest professional counseling to someone who is having trouble getting over heartbreak.)

- in the divorce rate

Here are some suggestions for how to make this cultural revolution happen:

- motivate people to put in the effort required to prepare themselves for a healthy relationship by becoming a strong person (that's what this book is trying to do)

- ask parents to consider encouraging their teen to become strong before they date and to only date another strong person

- ask parents to consider not allowing their teens below a freshman in high school to participate in group or one-on-one dating (as you read in Chapter 7 and 8 - the later a person starts dating, the better)

- ask parents to consider allowing only group dating of six or more while their teen is freshmen or sophomore in high school

- ask parents to consider allowing their high school teens to only date someone who's no more than two grade levels higher than their year in school (for example, a sophomore could date no higher than a senior - a junior could date no higher than a freshman in college, etc. The purpose of this suggestion is to protect teens from being taken advantage of by smooth talking older teens and young adults.)

- encourage the formation of a Strong Club™ at schools and in the community for the purpose of: 1. helping teens and young adults learn how to be strong by having good character, having a positive attitude, fulfilling their responsibilities, putting forth their best effort, and displaying self-control 2. encouraging teens and young adults to be strong 3. recognizing teens and young adults who are strong 4. giving teens and young adults a club where they feel that they belong, where they feel supported, where they can make real friends, where they have an opportunity to get to know others without dating, where they can participate in wholesome recreational activities, and where they can serve others.

- ask the "Y", other community organizations, and recreation departments to work together to provide wholesome and fun recreational activities for teens and young adults on Friday and Saturday nights throughout the year at a reasonable cost

- ask people who read this book to consider telling their friends and family about it in person and through social media (letting them know that free excerpts from the book can be found at truelovelasts.org), asking their local public library to purchase the book, wearing true love lasts.™ apparel, displaying a free true love lasts.™ bumper sticker on their car, writing a review of *True Love Lasts* on their favorite bookseller's website, and/or submitting a question about dating to the Strong Dating blog which can be found at strongdating.wordpress.com

FINAL WORD TO WOMEN

The lives of more and more women are spinning out of control. It's hard to believe that so many women around the world are dating before they're ready and are giving their bodies before marriage to someone else for fun, because they think they have true love for someone, because they think someone has true love for them, or because they hope they'll get true love from their boyfriend if they do. (I read an article in the newspaper that said about 33 out of every 100 (33%) of women in the United States become pregnant before the age of 20 . . . what a sad statistic for the women, but even more so for the children - many of whom will grow up without a constant strong loving father figure in their lives.)

Many women move from one dating relationship with sex to another searching for true love. They don't realize that they're looking for true love in all the wrong places. They don't realize that they're damaging their emotions. They don't realize that they're setting themselves up for a wide variety of life changing events such as:

- getting a sexually transmitted disease* (It's not a joke, it's a horrible problem - a government agency estimates that there are over 19 million new STD infections each year and about 50% of these infections are in teens and young adults. The agency also estimates that about 24,000 women in the United States become infertile each year because of an STD. There are 25 different STD's and 4 are incurable. Former U.S. Surgeon General C. Everett Koop said: "When you have sex with someone, you are having sex with everyone they have had sex with for the last ten years, and everyone they and their partners have had sex with for the last ten years.")

- becoming a mother without being married*

- being in an abusive relationship

- realizing that the person who you gave your body to doesn't have true love for you*

- realizing that you don't have true love for the person who you gave your body to*

- having an unloving unhappy marriage relationship*

- getting divorced*

I hope this book has given you good information and suggestions that you can use if you one day decide to try to develop and maintain a healthy relationship. I also hope that you'll decide to make becoming a strong person one of your main goals in life (if you're not already strong). And finally, I hope that you'll decide to have high standards for yourself and for the person who you choose to date.

Unfortunately strong men are hard to find - and a big part of the reason for this is that women's standards for who is acceptable dating material aren't high enough. It seems that many women are willing to date almost anyone they like or feel attracted to. Quite frankly, you need to be very selective about who you date because dating a weak man can severely damage your life - because this bad choice often leads to other bad choices including marrying a weak man. Many unhappily married and divorced women will tell you that it's better to be a lonely than it is to marry a weak man - because he will make your life miserable.

If more women are strong and have high standards for who they'll date - more men will become strong and the number of strong men available to date will increase. It's not easy to be a strong woman in today's society - but being a strong woman will help you to have the best possible life.

Have a great life!

*Please remember that if you've made bad choices in your life - nobody's perfect and it's never too late to change your ways and start trying to live your life as a strong person.

Please be sure to check out p. 109 for "21 tips that can help you to attract a strong person" and the Appendix starting on p. 111 for questions and answers about dating, a list of recommended books and other information.

Reflection: What's your reaction to the suggested cultural revolution? What parts of it do you agree with? What parts of it don't you agree with? What's the most important thing that you think needs to be done in order to make it happen?

"Have you ever noticed that wise people make careful choices - and that they're especially careful when making a bad choice could damage their life?"

Question: *"What should I do after I read True Love Lasts?"*

I hope that you'll put the information/suggestions you've read to good use. Many people who read the book realize that there are some attributes of a strong person that they need to work on and that now is a great time for them to start working on a daily basis to become a stronger and stronger person.

Some people who read the book realize that they need to put in the effort required to find a few strong real friends to go through life together with - friends who will help and encourage them to become a stronger person.

And finally, a good number of people who read the book decide to use the 21 tips for attracting a strong person on p. 109.

"The best way to attract the type of person that you want to date (a strong person) is to become the type of person that you want to date (a strong person)."

"It's OK if you don't agree with everything in this book - please just use what made sense to help you to have the best possible life."

FINAL WORD TO MEN

I hope this book has given you good information and suggestions that you can use if you one day decide to try to develop and maintain a healthy relationship. I also hope that you'll decide to make becoming a strong person one of your main goals in life (if you're not already strong). And finally, I hope that you'll decide to have high standards for yourself and for the person who you choose to date.

Here are some final words that you've probably already heard from someone but I need to make sure: You need to know that many women are selfish/immature and they desperately want someone to make them feel loved - someone to meet their emotional and other needs. Many will tell you almost anything (the most effective being "I love you") and are willing to give you their bodies before marriage in order to get what they want. I realize that no one likes to be told to "wake up," but you need to "wake up" to these facts before you fall into their trap.

Another thing you need to know is that strong women are hard to find - and a big part of the reason for this is that men's standards for who is acceptable dating material aren't high enough. It seems that many men are willing to date almost anyone with good looks. Quite frankly, you need to be very selective about who you date because dating a weak woman can severely damage your life - because this bad choice often leads to other bad choices including marrying a weak woman. Many unhappily married and divorced men will tell you that it's better to be a lonely than it is to marry a weak woman - because she will make your life miserable.*

If more men are strong and have high standards for who they'll date - more women will become strong and the number of strong women available to date will increase. It's not easy to be a strong man in today's society - but being a strong man will help you to have the best possible life.

Have a great life!

*Please remember that if you've made bad choices in your life - nobody's perfect and it's never too late to change your ways and start trying to live your life as a strong person.

Please be sure to check out p. 109 for "21 tips that can help you to attract a strong person" and the Appendix starting on p. 111 for questions and answers about dating, a list of recommended books, and other information.

Reflection: What's your reaction to the suggested cultural revolution? What parts of it do you agree with? What parts of it don't you agree with? What's the most important thing that you think needs to be done in order to make it happen?

"Let the wife make the husband glad to come home, and let him make her sorry to see him leave."
- Martin Luther

21 TIPS THAT COULD HELP YOU TO ATTRACT A STRONG PERSON

1. Take the time and put in the effort to become a strong person yourself (this is the most important tip)

2. Put yourself in as many situations as possible that will allow you to potentially come in contact with other strong people - community service organizations, the library, high school or college clubs, the "Y" or other workout facilities, religious book studies, coffee shops, non-alcoholic parties, bookstores, concerts (wear a good pair of earplugs to protect your ears from permanent hearing loss), co-ed recreational athletic teams, community service projects, mission trips, volunteer service, etc. Try to get to know other people as much as possible without dating

3. Be cheerful, approachable, and friendly - smile regularly to put others at ease (let people see your positive attitude)

4. Take a real interest in getting to know others. Ask people an open-ended question about themselves in order to get them talking. Share things related to what's been said as needed to keep the conversation going. Then ask them another question

5. Be polite and kind to everyone - even to people who you don't like or enjoy being around

6. If you decide to not accept a request for a date, do it in a kind way (being rude isn't a good choice and it doesn't help you - word about it will get out and you'll become less approachable)

7. Be confident about yourself - if you're trying to become a stronger person each day, you already have a lot going for you

8. Be humble - don't act like you're Miss Charming or you're Mr. Wonderful

9. Don't be too concerned about whether or not someone likes you

10. Have the attitude that if someone doesn't like you - they don't really know you

11. Take care of yourself by getting enough sleep (at least nine hours for teens, at least seven hours for adults according to the experts), exercising regularly (if approved by your doctor), and eating a healthy diet

12. Develop a good sense of humor - including the ability to laugh at your own mistakes

13. Be known as a hard worker

14. Dress well and dress modestly at the same time (wearing seductive clothing doesn't attract another strong person)

15. Pay attention to your appearance, but don't obsess over it. (remember that strong people are attracted to other strong people, they're not overly concerned about looks - because they realize that looks fade with age) If you use makeup, make sure it's not excessive. Use perfumes and colognes sparingly - if at all

16. Truly care about other people

17. Stay in close communication with real friends who can help you through the ups and downs of life and hold you accountable

18. Be patient - real friends can help you with this

19. Persevere - please remember that almost nothing worthwhile is quick and easy. Please don't settle for dating a weak person

20. Don't take it personally if someone doesn't want to date you

21. Don't act desperate for a date

APPENDIX

Dating questions and answers

In order to try to help people to make good dating choices, I've answered thousands of dating questions online and in person. The following are some of the most asked questions and answers. The wording has been changed to protect the identity of the asker. I hope that they'll help you to make good dating choices. If your appropriate question isn't listed, please ask it at the Strong Dating blog at strongdating.wordpress.com. (It usually takes several weeks for an answer to be posted.)

Q. Why do I need to read any information and suggestions about dating? I know what I'm doing and I want to make my own mistakes.

A. Of course it's a free country and you can do pretty much whatever you want unless it's against the law. However that doesn't mean that bad dating and marriage choices made without having good information won't have a negative effect upon your life and upon the lives of others (your significant other, children, parents, siblings, etc.). I encourage you to take the time to become as knowledgeable as possible about dating and marriage because the truth is that nobody knows it all. My opinion, based upon years of observation, is that people who put in the time and effort required to become really knowledgeable about dating and marriage are more likely to make good choices and are more likely to find true love.

Q. I like him, I think he likes me, and he's so cute. Should I ask him out?

A. Sorry, I know that it's old-fashioned, but my opinion is that this usually isn't a good idea. Some people may disagree - but I think that if he's a strong man, he'll take the initiative and ask you out.

I could be wrong, but it sounds like you're making dating choices mainly based upon whether someone likes you, you like them, and looks. Unfortunately this approach to dating, used by most people, usually leads to a broken heart.

May I suggest that the first question to ask yourself when considering whether or not to date someone is, "Is this person a strong person?" If they're not, no matter how much you like them, how much they like you, or how "cute" or "hot" they are, - please don't date them. A strong person has good character (honesty, integrity, trustworthiness), a positive attitude (cheerful, caring, friendly, forgiving, helpful, and respectful), fulfills their responsibilities (for handling pains in a positive way, for always trying to make a good choice, for taking care of themselves, for serving others), puts forth their best effort, and displays self-control (of their body, anger, tongue and money).

My suggestion is that you put in the effort necessary to become a strong person (if you're not already), forget about this guy unless he's a strong person, and eventually look for this type of guy (otherwise you are setting yourself up for a broken heart). Unfortunately this type of man is difficult to find - but save yourself the heartache and don't settle for less.

Please remember that you eventually want a 40, 50, or 60 year marriage - not a 5 or 10 year marriage.

Hope this helps!

Q. How do I get up the courage to ask a girl out?

A. It's natural to feel nervous when you're thinking about asking a strong woman out. I sure was. Pretty much everyone has the fear of rejection. I hope that this doesn't sound too harsh, but if you're having a big problem working up the courage to ask a strong woman out, it's possible that you need to work on becoming a stronger person before asking her out. My suggestion is that you wait until you're a strong man and you're at least a junior or senior in high school before asking a strong woman out on a one-on-one date (or at least a freshmen or sophomore for a group date). Practice what you're going to say and plan a good time to ask her in person. I know that rejection is tough for anyone to handle, but the goal is to become so strong as a person that you don't really care too much about what other people say, do, or think - and that includes a lady who says "no" when you ask her for a date.

Q. I'm 19 and I've never had a girlfriend. I feel like I'm so far behind my friends in terms of experience. I'm beginning to think that I'm going to be alone all my life. What should I do?

A. You are being way too hard on yourself. It's actually a good thing that you haven't had a girlfriend yet because it means that you've avoided having your heart broken. The best way to attract a strong woman is to become a strong man. (I also include a summary of the attributes of a strong person and the main tips for attracting a strong person in the answer.)

Q. We spend hours and hours talking on a social media site and texting. I've only met him in person once, but I think I'm starting to fall in love with him. What should I do?

A. First of all let me explain that when someone says that they are "falling in love" it usually means that a person is starting to have the feeling of being "in love" - instead of true love which is supposed to be a lifelong commitment. Please remember that having the feeling of being "in love" is relatively easy to get - while true love involves really getting to know another person and usually takes a long period of time to develop (often years).

Please keep in mind that it's easy for a person to hide what they are really like when they mainly communicate via social media and texting. Research shows that 75% of good communication between two people is actually nonverbal (body language, the expression on someone's face, etc.) which you don't get electronically. My suggestion is that you dramatically cut back on the time that you spend on social media and texting - and find a way to spend more time in face-to-face conversation with him as well as participating in a wide variety of wholesome activities together. This is the only way for you to get to know what he's really like and for him to get to know what you're really like. Be sure to pay special attention to how your significant other treats you and other people - and how he reacts when something goes wrong or he doesn't get what he wants.

Q. Could I possibly love someone I hardly know? I can't stop thinking about him.

A. It's highly unlikely that you have true love for someone you hardly know. It sounds like you have a bad case of infatuation. Infatuation is having the intense feeling of being "in love" very quickly - sometimes at first sight. True love is so much more than just having the feeling of being "in love" - it's supposed to be a mutual lifelong commitment. When you say that you love your significant other, you're saying that you're committed to loving them for the rest of your life. Please remember that true love lasts - it almost never fails.

Q. She dumped me. How can I get over her?

A. I'm really sorry about your heartache. One of the best ways to get over a woman is to become a strong man - if you're not one already. (I also include a summary of the attributes of a strong person in the answer.)

You may need some professional counseling to help you get over her. It's often available for a low fee through insurance.

Q. How do I know whether or not to continue in a dating relationship?

A. A decision of whether or not to continue in a dating relationship should be made after participating in a wide variety of wholesome activities together in order to carefully find out what the person you're dating is really like and to give the person you're dating an opportunity to find out what you're really like. Please remember that many people try to hide what they are really like by putting on an act during dating. Good reasons for breaking off a dating relationship in a kind way include: the other person not treating you and/or others with respect, the other person having a serious problem, the other person not having one or more of the attributes of a strong person, realizing that you don't have lots and lots in common after all, realizing that you don't think the same things are important in life, realizing the chemistry that you thought was there isn't there or realizing that this isn't the person you want to spend the rest of your life with.

Unfortunately way too many people stay in a dating relationship because they don't want to be without a boyfriend or girlfriend - instead of being strong and breaking up in a kind but firm way. It's better to be lonely than it is to be dating a person who you know isn't right for you.

Q. My boyfriend cheated on me, but I still love him. How do I get him back?

A. Unfortunately true love is supposed to be a mutual lifelong commitment. By cheating on you he's proven that he doesn't have true love for you. He's shown that he can't be trusted - and that most likely he will cheat on you again in the future. He's shown that he's not a strong person. I'm sorry to sound blunt - but why would you want this kind of guy back? Do you want to set yourself up for another broken heart in the future?

My suggestion is that you forget about this guy, become a strong person (if you're not already) and eventually look for a strong man. It's true that this type of guy is not easy to find, but please don't settle for less.

Please go to professional counseling if you need help getting over this guy.

Q. Is love a good enough reason to marry someone?

A. Unfortunately many times not. When you say love, I'm presuming that you mean true love - love that is supposed to be a lifelong commitment, instead of just having the feeling of being "in love." In addition to being sure that you have true love for each other, you need to ask yourselves questions like: Are both of you strong people? Do you have lots and lots of things in common? Is their strong chemistry between the two of you? Do you have similar goals for your life together? Are the same things in life important to both of you? Do you have very similar values? Have you treated each other and others with respect during your dating relationship? Are both of you hard workers? Are both of you free of serious problems? Do both of you agree that divorce is not even an option? How are you going to pay your bills if you decide to get married? Do both of you know how to control money? Do both of you want children? Do respected strong adults think that it's a good idea for you to get married? (I also include a summary of the attributes of a strong person in the answer.)

Q. Why should I put in the effort to try to live my life every day as a strong person?

A. Three important reasons - #1 Living your life as a strong person will help you to have the best possible life (living your life as a weak person just doesn't work - a person who doesn't have good character, who doesn't have a good attitude, who doesn't fulfill their responsibilities, who doesn't give their best effort, and who doesn't have self-control is not going to have the best possible life) #2 Strong people are more likely to find true love and to be able to give true love #3 Strong people are more likely to have a lifelong loving marriage if they decide to get married one day

Q. What's the best way to kiss my boyfriend in order to turn him on?

A. I wouldn't worry about it until you're married - you don't want things to get out of hand. (I also include some information about kissing from pp. 62-63 in the answer.)

Q. How do I make myself look more attractive to guys?

A. A strong guy is attracted to a hard working strong woman. Even though this type of guy isn't overly concerned with looks - it helps to pay attention to your appearance (but don't obsess), wear attractive modest clothing (strong guys are not attracted to girls who wear immodest clothing), exercise (if your doctor says it's OK), eat a good balanced diet that minimizes fats and sugars, and get your sleep (9-10 hours for teens and 7-8 hours for young adults).

"Any big goal worth going after (like becoming a strong person if you're not one already) is worth the work that it's going to take to achieve it."

Recommended books

The following books have been selected with the hope that they'll help you:

Group Dating: 301 Ideas by Blair Tolman, Tristan Tolman, and Kelli Weaver*

This book can spark your imagination for wholesome and fun group dating activities.

Fall in Love Stay in Love by Dr. Willard F. Harley, Jr.

This book will help you to learn how to keep the feeling of being "in love" at a high level after marriage.

We Can Work It Out: How to Solve Conflicts, Save Your Marriage by C. Notarius and Howard Markman

This book will help you to improve your communication skills.

The Money Book for the Young, Fabulous & Broke by Suze Orman

This book will help you to develop the crucial skill of being able to control your spending by living on a budget.

Getting Real: Helping Teens Find Their Future - by Kenneth Gray

This book, along with the website bls.gov, can help you to start the process of selecting a career with good job opportunities - a career that you will enjoy and that will allow you to support yourself and possibility one day a family.

If you have more dating questions

Please post your question at the Strong Dating Blog which can be accessed at strongdating.wordpress.com. Your question might help someone else to avoid making a bad dating choice, develop a healthy relationship, and to find true love.

Request for suggestions

Please feel free to let us know what you didn't agree with and/or your suggestions for improving the book (topics for additional chapters, more information needed in a particular chapter, more questions and answers needed at the end, etc.) by sending a e-mail to info@strongbookpublishing.com. We want to know! Your input may be used to improve future editions of the book. (Please do not include any names in your e-mail. Your e-mail address will not be shared with anyone.)

True Love Lasts T-shirts, etc.

Visit truelovelasts.org for more information about true love lasts.™ T-shirts and other merchandise.

Strong Clubs™

The purpose of Strong Clubs™ is to:

- help people learn how to be strong
- encourage people to be strong
- recognize people who are strong
- provide a club where people feel that they belong
- give people an opportunity to make real friends
- give people an opportunity to get to know each other without dating
- give people an opportunity to serve their community

The ABC's of Behavior™ (info from strongclubs.org)

<u>A</u>ggression - when a person tries to hurt others with their words or their body

<u>B</u>ad Choice - when a person chooses to make a bad choice even though they know it's a bad choice (often they're being selfish by doing what they feel like doing instead of what they know is a good choice)

<u>C</u>omplying - when a person chooses to make a good choice but only to avoid punishment or to get a reward

<u>S</u>trong - when a person chooses to make a good choice just because it's a good choice and they're not concerned about what weak others say, do, or think about their choice (They make the good choice of having good character, having a positive attitude, fulfilling their responsibilities, giving their best effort, and displaying self-control.)

A Strong Person C.A.R.E.S.™ (info from strongclubs.org)

<u>C</u>haracter, <u>A</u>ttitude, <u>R</u>esponsibility, <u>E</u>ffort, and <u>S</u>elf-control

(For more information about Strong Club™ school assemblies, or how to start a Strong Club™ at your school / in your community, please go to strongclubs.org. If you have additional questions, please send an e-mail to info@strongclubs.org.)

When you have a chance, please check out the following websites for the latest information:

TRUELOVELASTS.ORG

STRONGCLUBS.ORG

ABOUT THE AUTHOR

James Wegert has three college degrees and is certified as a school counselor, but he's learned the most from the School of Hard Knocks (making bad choices). Based upon his education and experience, he thinks that many teens and young adults don't have enough good information before, during, and after dating - and this lack of information makes it more likely that they'll mess up their lives by making bad dating choices. He wrote the book *True Love Lasts* in order to provide them with important information and suggestions about healthy relationships and things related to healthy relationships - and to encourage them to put in the effort required to become strong. He feels that people can maximize the possibility that they'll one day have a lifelong loving marriage if they're strong before dating and they use the Strong Dating™ approach to dating explained in this book. He's periodically available to give informative and somewhat humorous True Love Lasts™ presentations based upon the book to schools and to communities. The production of a DVD version of this presentation is being considered. The author can be contacted at info@truelovelasts.org.

ATTENTION - SCHOOLS, OTHER ORGANIZATIONS ETC.: Discounts are available on bulk orders of this book - please see p. 123 for the bulk order form. A preview copy of this book is available free upon request to principals, assistant principals, instructional supervisors, school counselors, and teachers who are considering having their students study this book by sending an e-mail to info@strongbookpublishing.org.

"You're in charge of creating your own reality. You can have the best possible life for yourself from now on by making the good choice to live your life as a strong person every day. If you fail to be strong one day by making a bad choice - that's OK - pick yourself up, dust yourself off, and try again the next day. Let there be no doubt - you can do this. Never ever give up trying to be a strong!"

BULK ORDER FORM

"Save by ordering in bulk direct from the publisher"

True Love Lasts books*:
7-29 copies - $5.50** per copy with free shipping
30-99 copies - $4.50** per copy with free shipping
(Please request a quote for quantities of 100 or more.)

# of books requested_____   Cost_____

true love lasts.™ (with a small TRUELOVELASTS.ORG underneath)
bumper stickers - 1 free with this page, additional stickers $2**

# of bumper stickers requested_____   Cost_____

PA residents add 6% tax or include
a copy of your tax exempt form   _____

                                        Total _____

Please send your first name and last initial, e-mail address, shipping address, and check/money order (made payable to Strong Book Publishing - information is never shared) to:

Strong Book Publishing
PO Box 5234
Lancaster, PA 17606-5234

*Single books can be purchased at createspace.com/4498133 or from your favorite bookseller.

**Prices are subject to change without notice. Please allow up to 3 weeks for delivery. If you have any questions, please e-mail us at info@strongbookpublishing.org. Thank you.

NOTES: